BUSINESS ETHICS

BUSINESS SERIES
Stanley F. Teele and David W. Ewing, Editors

BUSINESS ETHICS

THOMAS M. GARRETT
UNIVERSITY OF SCRANTON

NEW YORK
APPLETON-CENTURY-CROFTS
DIVISION OF MEREDITH PUBLISHING COMPANY

FOR FRANK CORBIN
WHO HAD MORE FAITH THAN I

Foreword

The Reverend Thomas M. Garrett, S.J., draws on an unusually rich and varied background for this study of ethics in business. A graduate of Gonzaga College in Spokane, Washington, he attended Weston College in Weston, Massachusetts, from 1952 to 1956, receiving the S.T.B. and the S.T.L. degrees. Cardinal Richard Cushing ordained him in 1955. From 1956 to 1960 he studied abroad—in France, Italy, Switzerland, and Germany. He received his Ph.D. in Philosophy from The Gregorian University in Rome. In addition to his theological studies, Father Garrett has worked in classical studies at Wernersville, Pennsylvania, and in philosophy at Woodstock College; for two years he taught classical languages at Georgetown University; and during his stay at Fribourg, Switzerland, he studied economics. In the United States he has won respect as a thoughtful writer of books and articles on questions of advertising, automation, and television.

When we began our conversations with Father Garrett about this book, in 1964, he was at The University of Scranton as Director of the Institute on Business and Social Ethics. In 1965 he came to the Cambridge Center for Social Studies and finished this text there in 1966. He has now returned to The University of Scranton.

This volume is one of a series of original paperback texts by eminent authorities on business administration. Like its companion books, it is designed for use in business school courses and in-company training programs. Instructors can use it either as a basic text or as a supplementary text, *viz.*, part of the "package" of teaching materials used in their courses. The author has sought to distill a large mass of material into the comparatively brief space of this

v

120255

book. It represents a compact analysis of highlights and key topics only. Hence businessmen, too, should find it useful in enlarging their understanding of management problems.

S. F. Teele and D. W. Ewing

Preface

This book is designed primarily for students and those who have just begun a career in business. It does not provide an extended or detailed treatment of the social ethics of business, although frequent mention is made of the social dimension. The reason is simple. The young man in business does not have to make decisions in these areas, although he should be aware that he will have to face social problems as he advances. Those interested in these broader social questions should refer to the readings suggested throughout the book.

The introductory character of the book is evident not only in the delineation of subject matter but in the method of presentation and in the simplified ethical theory which is provided. No attempt has been made to present a fully developed ethics which could be used in the study of problems of medicine and family life as well as in business. Rather, I have limited myself to a simple set of basic principles adequate for the problems met by beginners in business ethics. In other words, the theory is tailored to the purposes of this book and to the problems it studies.

In general, the reader will find no detailed catalogue of regulations, nor an exhaustive treatment of the topics selected for study. Our purpose has been to supply a minimum framework of business ethics and a method of analyzing problems. If the book sensitizes the reader to relevant ethical values and the way in which they can be brought to bear on concrete problems, it will have succeeded.

There are cynics who doubt the utility and feasibility of even such modest aims as those listed above. The author, however, writes with profound convictions based on considerable contact with businessmen. He is convinced that Americans agree on more points of ethics than one suspects and that most businessmen want to do the right thing. He also believes that most of them will do the right thing if given a little intelligent and realistic encouragement. While much of the current interest in business ethics may be motivated by self-interest or public pressures, it has more profound roots. The enlightened businessman is sensitive to the dignity of his own work, the needs of his employees and of society. He wants to work out solutions that serve all legitimate interests. He wants to make his world more meaningful.

It should be obvious that the amateur or the incompetent in business cannot live up to either the demands of business or the demands of ethics. It is hoped, then, that these pages will encourage not only ethical reflection but the study of business and business problems. Teachers in a variety of business courses will find that the matter can be used to introduce the student to the ethical dimension and to some of the problems in business which urgently need solution. In particular, these pages may convince the beginner that business is not a fixed and unchangeable reality, but part of a rapidly changing world that not only creates problems but offers an opportunity for technical brilliance and human creativity on the highest level.

Because the strict space limitation of this book precluded proper documentation, I have not used notes to support my ideas, but to show the reader where he can find more information on the topic. The notes, then, serve as a brief classified bibliography.

ACKNOWLEDGMENTS

Most authors are brain-pickers, and I am no exception. Indeed, I sometimes feel that I am no more than a compiler of the ideas of others who lack the time to organize or write down their own thoughts. In any event, this book owes a great deal to those who read and criticized preliminary drafts as well as to those who have helped me to further clarify my thinking. My greatest debt is to Thomas McMahon, Professor of Moral Theology of the Viatorian Seminary in Washington, D.C. An expert in his own right, he spent long hours helping me to rethink nearly every page of this work. David Ewing of the *Harvard Business Review,* Luke Powers of Saint Bonaventure's University, and Austin Boulay of Boulay and Co., Certified Public Accounts, also criticised substantial portions. I have not always adopted their suggestions, but neither have I discarded them without full consideration.

Both Professor Joseph Kleiner of the University of Wisconsin and Mr. Sid Bernstein of *Advertising Age* supplied me with valuable case materials. Mickey Garrett and Edward Gordon helped me considerably by raising numerous problems faced by the beginner in business. My greatest stimulation, however, came from my students in the Honors Program at the University of Scranton and in the Management Training Program of the Western Electric Company. They taught me how vague even a well-intentioned writer can be if he is not aware of his audience. If I have not profited completely from their lessons, the blame is certainly mine.

Finally, thanks are due to three people who gave me the courage to go on when I suffered doubts about the usefulness of what I was doing. Frank Corbin, of Burke-Corbin Associates, prodded me constantly with the result that this book is dedicated to his faith. Reverend Edward Sponga, S.J., President of the University of Scranton encouraged me and supplied me with time and secretarial help. My secretary, Mrs. Thomas Evanko, not only typed and checked references, but gave me considerable insight into the ethical problems faced by the rank-and-file employee in a variety of businesses.

Finally, I wish to express my gratitude to the companies and publishers who gave me permission to cite material. Others desirous of using the same material should consult the copyright holders mentioned in the footnotes.

T.M.G.

Contents

I

Basic Theory

1

Some Basic Principles

INTRODUCTION

The word ethics is used in a rather precise sense throughout this book.[1] It is important, then, to define the word and to distinguish it from terms with which it has sometimes been identified. Ethics is *not* the study of morals, whether this word is used to designate conformity to conventional social rules or the existing moral judgments of men. Although existing norms and judgments may contain valuable insights, ethics does *not* accept them, but sets out to criticize and test them in terms of more ultimate norms. To put it another way, custom, convention and the accepted courtesies of a society are *not* the foundations of ethics even though they can provide valuable hints as to what men think. For this reason, business ethics must study existing business codes to determine whether they have a solid foundation or only express a narrow consensus of a group or a sort of commercial etiquette.

Law enshrines many of the ethical judgments of a society, but it is *not* coextensive with ethics. In the first place, law is generally

---

[1] A fuller development of the ethical theory given in this chapter will appear in my new book, *Problems and Perspectives in Ethics,* to be published by Sheed & Ward, in 1966. Different, but not necessarily conflicting aproaches can be found in Philip W. Van Vlaak, *Management Ethics Guide* (Brookings, South Dakota, South Dakota State University Press, 1964); Henry J. Wirtenberger, S.J., *Morality and Business* (Chicago, Loyola University Press, 1962), and Herbert Johnston, *Business Ethics,* 2nd ed. (New York, Pitman, 1961).

concerned only with the minimum regulation necessary for public order, while ethics examines both the individual and the social good in all dimensions. In the second place, ethics criticizes law as it does custom in an effort to obtain more perfect rules for the conduct of life. While the law demands great respect, it too is subject to the higher norms which ethics seeks to develop.

Although some will dispute the statement, ethics is *not* even identical with religious morality or moral theology. The great religions derive their moral precepts not only from human experience but from divine revelation. Ethics must rely on the unaided human reason. Because of this, the conclusions of ethics often fall far short of the ethical imperatives found in both Judaism and Christianity. Yet, there should be no conflict between ethics and moral theology, for ethics admits its incompleteness and sends the religious man to his faith for the completion of his moral equipment. No one should be surprised, then, if this short book does not use all the resources and equipment of the great religious traditions in moral science.

Since many people identify ethics with vague feelings of approval or disapproval, it should be noted that ethics does *not* rest on feelings but on the careful examination of the reality around us. It may be unpleasant to fire a man, but ethics may demand just this. It may be hard to do the right thing in the face of strong disapproval and at great personal cost, but principles and not emotions should guide us. With all of these things in mind, we can now make some more positive statements about the nature of ethics.

Ethics is the science of judging specifically human ends and the relationship of means to those ends. In some way it is also *the art of controlling means so that they will serve specifically human ends.* From this point of view, ethics involves the use of any human knowledge whatsoever which has something to tell us about the relations between men or about the suitability of the available instruments. As an art, moreover, it involves techniques of judging and decision-making as well as the tools of social control and personal development. Thus ethics really is or should be involved in all human activities.

Business ethics is concerned primarily with the relationship of business goals and techniques to specifically human ends.[2] It studies

_____

[2] Those interested in the full scope of business ethics should at least scan the following books and collections of articles. Annals of the American Academy of

the impacts of acts on the good of the individual, the firm, the business community, and society as a whole. While it does not concentrate on the obligations which man has as a private individual and a citizen, these enter in, since the businessman is not three separate persons. This means that business ethics studies the special obligations which a man and a citizen accepts when he becomes a part of the world of commerce.

The social dimension of business ethics must not be overlooked since many major problems arise from the relationship of business to the broader society. Often, as we shall see towards the end of this book, business is involved in social situations which harm men or breed injustice even though business alone is not responsible for this. Unless we recognize this social dimension from the very start, there is danger of reducing business ethics to a study of only individual relationships between men. This would simplify the work at hand, but only by robbing business of its full human significance.

SPECIFICALLY HUMAN ENDS

In speaking of specifically human ends, we must avoid a narrow point of view. Men are complex beings existing in an extremely complex world. While we may be tempted to work out some simple answers, experience shows us that such answers are not only frustrating, but at odds with the way people actually see themselves. Man is not merely a creature made for power or pleasure. He wants and is made for more than this. He is not purely and simply a social being but has a worth and dignity as an individual. All aspects of man enter into ethics. The problems, of course, arise when we have to harmonize the seeming conflicts between man's various roles. This may be difficult, but dodging the issue does not solve the problem.

Political and Social Sciences, *Ethics in Business*, Vol. 343 (September, 1962); Robert Bartels, ed., *Ethics in Business* (Columbus, Ohio, Ohio State University Press, 1963); Howard R. Bowen, *Social Responsibilities of the Businessman* (Harper & Row, 1953); J. W. Bunting, ed., *Ethics of Modern Business Practice* (Philadelphia, Prentice-Hall, 1953); Thomas M. Garrett, S.J., *Ethics in Business* (New York, Sheed, 1963); William T. Greenwood, ed., *Issues in Business and Society* (Boston, Houghton Mifflin, 1964); George Albert Smith, Jr., *Business, Society and the Individual* (Homewood, Illinois, Irwin, 1962); Joseph W. Towle, ed., *Ethics and Standards in American Business* (Boston, Houghton Mifflin, 1964).

Since this is not a book in general ethical theory, I shall merely present a brief, but broad view of the specifically human ends in ethics. Because this view coincides in a large part with the American political tradition and with the teaching of great religions as well as with the view of a large number of modern philosophers, it is hoped that the reader will at least accept it as a working hypothesis.

The specifically human goal is the full human perfection of the human being as person. This means that the person is not a means to the perfection of society, the state or anything else. In this view, societies are means to the real perfection of the individual even though they may contribute to this only indirectly. Societies, of course, are very important means, and the individual who harms a social good can injure countless individuals. It is important, then, to make careful distinctions lest individuals think that societies exist for them alone and not for all individuals. Although the person as a person is to be treated as an end, some of his possessions, talents and activities must be subordinated to others. An individual's work, for example, may be used as a means to the good of a company providing that personal dignity and essential well-being are respected. So too, a man's time and wealth may have to be sacrificed to society so long as the person himself is not reduced to a mere thing. The full significance of this will emerge as we develop the difference between the necessary and useful goods and the major and minor evils which can occur in human life.

There are gray areas where it is difficult to say whether or not the person or merely some accidental aspect is being used as a means. However, reflection and experience can clarify these areas or at least reduce them to manageable dimensions. One hundred years ago we could not see clearly that most forms of segregation were really insults to basic human dignity. Today most intelligent people see the evil of segregation quite clearly. Similarly, there was a time when employers considered any contract as just, even though it might involve the brutalization of the worker and his family. Thus, ethics has as one of its functions the sharpening of our knowledge about the work practices affecting the dignity of the individual human being.

It should be noted that much unethical activity is rooted in a lack of respect for our own personal dignity. The man who sees his worth as identical with his earning power will tend to look at everyone else in the same way. The result is often a neglect of the rights of those who must work with or for him. Concretely, then, an understanding of ethics demands an appreciation of what it means to be truly human. This understanding is not easily attained, for momentary desires and narrow views of self-interest blind man not only to his own best advantage, but to the rights of others and to the exigencies of the societies of which he is a part and to which he owes so much. If a man does not have this breadth of vision, this book cannot give it to him. At very best, a book can only enlarge one's outlook a little and show how the basic respect for man is to be expressed in actual business situations.

Those who have a fairly complete idea of what it means to be a man will see at once why it is necessary to be ethical and to study ethics. The reason is not that good ethics and good business always coincide. Business efficiency, after all, is only one part of life. The reason is ultimately found in the fact that both the study and practice of ethics contribute to our growth as men and to the growth of society as a fit place for men to exist. Unless we have an ethics that puts business into the total framework of both individual and social life, we may end up as "successful" businessmen but mediocre, if not morally crippled, persons. Since mere instinct and vague good will are not enough to guide us in the complicated world around us, the study of goals and means is necessary.

RESPONSIBILTY IN A GENERAL SENSE

Whatever hurts the individual or the institutions necessary for his growth may be looked upon as an evil in some way. Similarly, whatever truly promotes the growth of the individual and the means available to him, is a good. Such simple statements, though true, will not solve our ethical problems. Nearly everything we do has some harmful impact on ourselves or others. If we were responsible for all the evil that flowed from our activities, whether foreseen or not, we would despair of ever being ethical. Even the most conscientious advertiser knows that some silly people will be deceived by his carefully written copy. Is he on that account unethical? Similarly, the employer who must fire an incompetent knows that the man's family will suffer. Is he responsible for these effects?

The answers to these questions are found in the very traditional ethical theory which states that "man is responsible at least for what he freely wills whether as a means or an end." To a large extent, this theory is found in civil law as well as in ethics. Someone may ask, however, if this means that I have no responsibility for the evils which I foresee will flow from my actions as necessary, probable or possible effects. Is a drug manufacturer who foresees that some people will be killed by his drug excused from all responsibility on the grounds that he does not will their death as a means or an end? The answer is obviously no, for both common sense and ethical theory recognize some obligation to avoid even unintended evil consequences in some circumstances. Where, then, do we draw the line?

TYPES OF EVIL AND CONSEQUENCES

At the very start, we must recognize that there are different types of evil consequences. Some evils strike at the very dignity of the human being or at means which are necessary for human growth. If I destroy a man's health so that he cannot work, I have done him a serious harm. On the other hand, there are evils which destroy goods which are only useful. Thus if a man loses a job, he has not in most cases lost his livelihood completely. It would appear to be simple common sense that the greater the foreseen, but unintended harm, the more responsible a person is liable to be. However, if I am responsible for all the evil, though unintended effects of my actions, life would be impossible.

In an attempt to solve this problem without falling into the vicious theory that the end justifies the means, writers on ethics have evolved the following principles. First, I am responsible for whatever I will as a means or an end. *If both the means and the end I am willing are good in and of themselves, I may ethically permit or risk the foreseen but unwilled side effects if, and only if, I have a proportionate reason for doing so.* To put it another way, I am not responsible for unwilled side effects if I have a sufficient reason for risking or permitting them, granted always that what I do will as a means or an end is good.

This principle is so crucial that it needs considerable explanation if it is to be used properly and not as a cover-up for unethical conduct. It does not imply that the end justifies the means, for the means willed must be good before the principle can be used. I cannot use it to justify deliberately killing an innocent man even if this would save thousands of lives. I cannot steal another man's property even though this will enable me to make millions of dollars. At best, the end can supply me with a sufficient reason for permitting or risking *side effects which are not means* to the end. I may catch pneumonia by diving into an icy stream in order to rescue a child, but the pneumonia does not help me to rescue the child. It is not a means and may be permitted or risked for such a serious reason.

The words *permitted* and *risked* have a precise meaning which reinforces what has been said above. I permit an evil when I foresee it as *certain* but do not will it as either a means or an end. I risk an evil when I foresee it as *probable* but do not will it as either a means or an end. In short, there is no question of risking or permitting what is willed as means or end. When in doubt, ask yourself whether you can obtain your end even if some miracle would stop the evil side effects. If the answer is yes, the evil is probably not a means. If the answer is no, the evil is a means and the principle of proportionality or limited responsibility does not apply.

Honest businessmen use this principle constantly. The advertiser who has prepared his copy carefully foresees that a few stupid people will misread it. He is not unethical, however, for he does not will their stupidity, and the service he renders to thousands allows him to permit the stupid to suffer. It would be quite different, of course, if he willed to deceive them as a means to keeping his business going. In such a case he can have no proportionate reason because he is using an evil act as a means.

The principle given above is still very crude. It needs to be refined if it is to be truly useful in making decisions. In the first place, it is necessary to have more precise norms on judging proportionality. In the second place, it is necessary to investigate more carefully a special case involving minor evils.

PROPORTIONALITY

Proportionality is to be judged by:
1. The type of goodness or evil involved.
2. The urgency of the situation.

3. The certainty or probability of the effects.
4. The intensity of one's influence on the effects.
5. The availability of alternate means.

In the abstract, a necessary good will outweigh a merely useful good. The more necessary will take precedence over the less necessary. For example, something necessary to keep a business in existence will take precedence over a cut in the ordinary dividend. Note that the hardship worked on some stockholders is not a means since of itself it does not help the company.

In the concrete, necessity is influenced by the urgency of the situation. Thus, staying in business today involves both research and the ability to meet one's payroll. However, since research can be postponed without irreparable harm, it would take second place to meeting the payroll because both the company and the employees depend on this for their existence.

The *certitude or probability of an effect* must be considered since a serious harm which is only slightly probable can clearly be outweighed by a certain good. Every major business innovation involves some risk of serious financial loss. The risk can be justified, however, if careful calculations indicate a high probability of increased growth. So too, work involving the risk of physical harm can be justified by the necessity of earning a living. Note that the risk of physical harm is not a means but is undesired by everyone.

The *intensity of one's influence* must be considered since often something or someone else is the major cause of the evil side effect. In firing a man for absenteeism, the employer foresees some hardship in the family. The major cause is not the employer but the employee whose faults created the situation. When one's influence is minimal, it does not require a very great good to justify permitting the side effects. Here again the hardship worked on the family is not a means for it does not help the company at all.

All of these *factors must be considered together* in making a judgment about proportionality. In general, one can start with the first factor and work his way down to the last, totaling up the factors at the end. Sometimes even this method will not yield an absolutely clear decision, but it will at least narrow the area of doubt.

The availability of alternate means must be considered. If the good effects can be obtained by a method which involves lesser evils or no evil side effects, it would be irrational and therefore unethical not to choose the alternate means, all other things being equal. One does not fire a worker if some lesser disciplinary action will produce the desired results, nor does a man permit others to be deceived if a little extra work will remove the cause of the deception. It would be irrational and unethical to continue an economic system which was inefficient when it was possible to work toward a better system which cost no more. This means that the possibility of alternatives which realize the good with fewer unwanted side effects can create an obligation to work towards this system. The *status quo* is not a perpetual excuse for permitting evils that can be eliminated.

MINOR EVILS OR PHYSICAL EVILS

The principle of proportionality applies to the risking or permitting evils of all sorts. It can be used only when what is willed as means or end is good. What, however, are we to say of the following cases where common sense tells us the act is ethical even though it involves willing some evil for a proportionate reason.

A parent spanks his child in order to teach him that stoves burn. An employer docks the wages of someone who is consistently tardy in the hope that the loss will reform the worker. The government destroys millions of tons of wheat to support prices. In each case an evil, the destruction of good, is willed. In each case most will feel that there is a proportionate reason for doing so. Does the end justify the means in these cases?

Writers on ethics have attempted to solve this problem in various ways. Many distinguish between a *physical evil,* which can be willed for a proportionate reason since it does not harm the dignity of man, and a *moral evil,* which involves willing something which is at odds with that dignity. This distinction is useful if one remembers that more than a physical evil is involved when the rights of others are involved. Thus I cannot steal another's property on the ground that the money is only a physical good and its loss only a physical evil. A doctor cannot cut off a man's arm to save his life if the man objects.

It is also possible to distinguish between *major evils,* which involve the destruction of goods necessary for an individual or society as well as the violation of rights, and *minor evils,* which involve harm to a purely physical good or to some means that is useful but not necessary for the individual and society. This distinction, too, is not without its difficulties, for Americans tend to evaluate things in quantitative terms whereas rights are qualitative. Furthermore, whether one uses the distinction between physical and moral evils or between major and minor evils, it may take years of study to determine the exact nature of some acts and effects. Indeed, much of this book is an attempt to decide what evils are major and therefore unethical when willed as means or ends.

No matter what distinction or terminology is used we can say: It is unethical to will a major or a moral evil either as a means or an end. Secondly, a physical or a minor evil cannot only be permitted or risked, but can even be willed as a means if there is a proportionate reason. The reason is that the physical or minor evil by definition does not go against the essential dignity of man but promotes it when there is a proportionate reason. As a result, the physical or minor evil is really not a full-fledged evil in many situations.

PROBLEMS

In the world of business, as elsewhere in human life, it can often be difficult to decide whether we are dealing with a major or minor evil. In addition, there is the danger of considering any harm done to others as minor and any good for ourselves as absolutely necessary. As a result, good ethics demands that the individual make a continual effort to arrive at objective evaluations of the effects of his acts on individuals and societies. The neglect of this obligation is certainly a source of much unethical conduct and might also be considered a major problem in ethics.

A few examples will help to illustrate the dangers of subjectivism divorced from objective considerations. An employer is installing a new process which is very dangerous. There are safety measures available, but he does not use them, since their cost will reduce his profits which will be higher than the industry average. Here we are dealing with an unethical act, since the potential harm outweighs the loss of some profits. One might be tempted to call the risk to life a purely physical evil, but it is more than this since workers have a right not to be *unnecessarily* exposed to risk, while a company has no right to a profit, let alone a high profit, gained by exposing others to unreasonable risks.

A young accountant tampers with his records to conceal his own mistakes. This fudging will almost certainly lead to costly errors being made. He argues that he will lose his job if caught and so is therefore ethically justified. Actually, there is no question of risking or permitting here, since he is willing an evil as a means. Furthermore, by his contract, he has agreed to take the consequences of his mistakes. Finally, the harm to the company would outweigh the harm to himself even if he were not using an unethical means to escape penalties. Even if the harm to the company were relatively small in terms of dollar losses, the employee is violating his contract which gave the company a right to honest work. Injuries to contracts are not minor, for the whole fabric of business and society depends on their sacredness. For all of these reasons, the young accountant is doing something unethical, no matter what his own rationalizations may be.

Additional dangers of self-deception exist when the impacts of an act are not directly visible and so not ordinarily considered. This is particularly true of the harmful effects on the spirit of society as a whole or on the morale of a company. A company may not see the hardship worked on people by the cumulative effect of over-pricing or false advertising, but it is there and must be considered. It may be difficult to estimate the effect of a plant relocation on a local community, but it cannot be disregarded as a minor consideration.

Law, custom, and public opinion do not completely determine the ethicality of our actions since they are more liable to be concerned with minimal requirements than with the complete situation. However, all three can be valuable in arriving at an evaluation of impacts. In addition, they can help the businessman escape some of his very natural bias.

Law in particular is important, since it enshrines the careful thinking of society's best representatives. At times it may be out of date since law often lags behind the developing social situation. However, although the law may permit things which are unethical, in general what it forbids is also forbidden by sound ethical thinking. For these reasons the study of business law and consultation with lawyers should be considered as a necessary preliminary in most areas of business ethics. If later chapters do not give complete summaries of the law on given points, it is because a short book must assume that the reader has other sources of information.

While trade customs often embody the results of sound ethical theory, they must be examined with care. The custom may have developed to protect the interests of only one group involved in business with the result that sometimes they sanction or even command acts which may be harmful to other groups. Thus although untruthful comparisons of products are unethical, advertising which avoids all meaningful comparisons with competing products is certainly not in the best interests of the consumer. No matter what the custom in the area, the ethical businessman will want to examine it for all of its implications.

Public opinion too, needs to be studied carefully. Often it condemns or approves certain business practices because it is unaware of the real issues involved. At the same time, it will often indicate to the ethical businessman that he has overlooked some relevant factor. The same remarks apply even to the writings of the "professional" critics of business who, though often ill-informed, may have something valuable to say.

Summary

What we have said above may be summed up in the following:

1. It is unethical to will a major evil to another or to one's self whether this evil be a means or an end.
2. It is unethical to risk or permit a major evil to another or to one's self without a proportionate reason. A proportionate reason exists when the good willed as means or end equals or outweighs the harmful side effects which are not willed as either means or end.
3. It is unethical to will, risk, or permit a minor evil without a proportionate reason.

POSITIVE OBLIGATIONS

The brief statements made above provide analytic tools for the determination of what we must avoid as unethical. In addition, we have positive obligations, that is, duties to bring something into existence. In a most general sense, we have a positive obligation when something is necessary for our own human perfection, the dignity of others, or the necessary operations of society. These obligations or duties are not absolute since the urgency of one may cause the postponement of another. In more general language, an individual may often have proportionate reasons for not fulfilling a positive obligation at a given moment. This makes positive obligations very different from the negative obligation to avoid all unethical acts as defined above. Thus, the extreme need of workers for their wages may excuse a manager temporarily from paying a dividend. The obligation to pay wages at a certain level may even be mitigated by the obligation to keep the business in existence, since the firm may be necessary for at least the subsistence of a large number of people. Because each general and particular situation must be judged in terms of the four factors covering proportionality, more general rules cannot be given at this time. It should be obvious, however, that positive obligations are limited by the following factors.

I am not obliged to do a good act whose harmful side-effects outweigh the good effects I intend. Indeed, I am forbidden to do such an act, since I have no proportionate reason for permitting the harm. A man is thus not obliged to raise wages when this will destroy the firm and put hundreds out of work within a short time.

I am not obliged to help someone who will not help himself, although I may do so if I desire. A company does not have to keep an employee who refuses to get proper medical care or to follow company regulations. A firm may have no obligation to contribute to local institutions if these are badly run.

I am not obliged to perform a positive good act if someone else has a more primary obligation and is willing and able to fulfill it. A firm, for example, is not obliged to provide for the education of workers' children since the workers and the government are in charge of this. Obligations, in other words, do not come into existence merely because there is a need, but they are assigned according to some system. As we shall see in later chapters, many problems in business ethics have their roots in the fact that society has assigned no one to take care of certain necessary activities.

RIGHTS

The term rights will be used frequently in the following pages. It derives its meaning from what has been said above. Basically, a right is a claim on other people. It arises from the relationship of the individual to some good which is either necessary or useful for his perfection. Since we are all men, these claims must be respected, for we cannot disregard another's good without in some way injuring ourselves. Rights, however, are not all of a piece, nor are they unlimited. In a general sense, we can distinguish between quasi-absolute rights, which are claims to things which man needs in order to be a man, and relative rights, which are claims not to be unreasonably impeded in the pursuit of even useful goods. While it is not always easy to differentiate between these in the concrete, the theoretical distinction is a useful analytic tool.

A man who is forced to work twelve hours a day, seven days a week, can hardly be human in the long run. To force him into such a situation is to violate his right to be treated as a human being. On the other hand, requiring men to appear for work at a given hour may limit the search for some useful good like an extra hour of sleep, but it is a reasonable limitation which does not make the worker less of a man. It is reasonable to make workers wear safety helmets even though they may dislike hats. It is unreasonable and a violation of freedom to make workers in an office wear hats. These examples are trivial, but it must be remembered that freedom is a good, and one needs a proportionate reason for limiting it.

It may be difficult to determine the exact limits of a right. On the surface, the violation of a right may appear to be no more than a slight injury to the feelings, property, or freedom of another. In reality, the violation of a right involves the denial of the claims of human dignity. It involves placing some mere thing or desire above the human person. Since all of us have basically the same nature, I harm myself when I harm another. I twist my sense of values when I disregard rights, and in the long run, this can destroy me as a human being no matter how much I may appear to gain by the careless and ruthless refusal to consider the claims of other men.

Some rights are inborn; a man has them merely because he is a man. The right to life is a prime example. Other rights, however, come into existence only when some act has created a title to a particular thing. A man has a right to a plot of land only if he has bought it, received it as a gift, or received it as a part of an inheritence. Similarly, in most cases a man has a right to a *particular* job only after a contract has been made. This point is extremely important, for although a man may have a right to work, no particular individual has a corresponding obligation to employ him. In short, there are some rights which are claims against society as a whole rather than against particular individuals. When this fact is overlooked, serious harm can be done by trying to force obligations on people against all reason. Only society itself can ultimately decide which individual, if any, must fulfill these claims against society itself. Often the assignment is made by law, but as we shall see, it can often be made by ratifying the acts of private individuals and firms who freely decide to undertake the job.

The exercise of rights, whether absolute or relative, is limited by the rights of others and by my obligation to respect them as well as by my obligation to respect myself. A man may own a house, but he has no right to burn it down when this would endanger his neighbors. Even if there were no neighbors, he would be limited by the obligation to use material things intelligently. An employer has a right to hire whom he will, but this is limited by his obligation to respect the human dignity of others A man has a right to life, but he may not save his own life by killing an innocent person. A company has a right to trade, but it has no right to exploit its customers. In short, the exercise of rights involves us in the concrete world where concrete possibilities as well as the rights of others limit the legitimate extent of our own claims. To put it another way, my obligation to respect others conditions my legitimate claims to things and on people.

COOPERATION IN EVIL

Many cases in business ethics involve cooperation in evil. When this cooperation includes willing the evil, either as a means or an end, this is an unethical act, except in those cases where there is a proportionate reason for willing a minor or physical harm.

At times, however, a person can be involved in a situation against his will. If he does not will the evil either as a means or an end, he may have a proportionate reason for risking or permitting harm. For example, the secretary who is typing up fraudulent reports is cooperating in an unethical act. Ordinarily she does not want others to be deceived or to profit from it. Further, if there is little that she can do to stop the harm while she needs the job, she can continue to do the physical work of typing. Since many cases of this type will appear frequently later on, it will suffice to say that the same basic principles apply here as elsewhere in ethics.

A treatment of the power of example is important in business ethics, for studies have shown that the example of the superior or supervisor is very significant for the other workers.[3] As a result, bosses must see that their acts do not encourage others to engage in unethical conduct. This is a delicate situation, for harm may be done if the employee misinterprets even an innocent act. Often, then, it is necessary to avoid both unethical conduct and the appearance of it. It should be clear, however, that when the superior's act is actually ethical, he can permit or risk the harm for a proportionate reason. After all, the stupidity of others does not create an absolute claim on the behavior of a man of true good will.

LOCATION OF RESPONSIBILITY

Our remarks about cooperation and bad example should make it clear that we can be partially responsible for actions whose primary cause is found elsewhere. Even though another may bear the major responsibility, I can share in it. Adolph Eichmann was responsible for his acts even though Hitler gave the orders and common soldiers performed the actual murders. In short, the ignoble art of buck-passing should not obscure the fact that we are responsible for our share of the evil when we risk it or permit it without a proportionate reason.

Often, to be sure, we are in a position where we cannot prevent evil or can prevent it only at a disproportionate price. In such situations, we may be excused temporarily. More often than not, the ob-

---

[3] Raymond C. Baumhart, S.J., "How Ethical Are Businessmen?" *Harvard Business Review*, Vol. 39, No. 4 (July-August, 1961).

ligation is transformed into the duty to work for the correction of the underlying situation. A minor employee often has no way of stopping his superior from stealing, but he can make the thefts more difficult. In these cases where he cannot stop the evil, he is at least obliged to mitigate it.

THE GRAY AREAS

There are gray areas in business ethics as in the rest of life. Neither our knowledge of the facts nor our analytic tools are accurate enough to solve all problems immediately and clearly. Despite this, ethics can help us in reaching correct decisions in the vast majority of cases. The science of ethics, then, has very high utility even though it is not perfect. The gray areas themselves are not excuses for unethical conduct so much as challenges to our intelligence. Thought and study can remove much of the darkness and narrow the gray areas to a very small proportion of life. Indeed, because intelligence is one of the necessary means to the perfection of the individual and society, we have a real obligation to study ethics and to bring the murky areas into the light of reason. Progress may be slow here as elsewhere, but the difficulty of the job does not excuse us forever.

PRACTICAL APPLICATION

The beginner in ethics is often confused by the array of factors which must be considered in making judgments about the ethicality of an act. While only experience and practice can eliminate most of the difficulties, systematic procedures are a great help. The procedure given below will lead to orderly habits of ethical analysis.

The following case can be used as an example. Your solution and reasoning can then be checked against the author's analysis. The XYZ company operating in the days before the Federal Drug Administration wants to market a new sleeping pill. Since the company is in bad financial condition after investing some two million dollars to develop the drug, the directors want to rush the promotion to the general public. Research indicates that the drug, though effective, has harmful side effects on unborn children. The company decides to go ahead anyway and puts on a small label saying, "Not to be used by pregnant women." The directors feel that this is enough warning. If they use more controls they feel that they will have to close the company and put some five hundred people out of work, or merge with a larger company which has been trying to buy them up for some time.

NEGATIVE OBLIGATIONS

Stage 1.
a. What is willed as a means and as an end?
b. What objective evil or good results from or is found in the means and the end?

Decision 1.
a. If a major evil is willed either as a means or an end, the analysis stops at this point. You are dealing with a clearly unethical act.

NOTE: A major evil robs a man of a quasi-absolute right or goes against his basic dignity. A major evil also exists when harm is done to a necessary social good.

b. If the above is not true, go on to stage two.

Stage 2.
a. What are the side effects which are *foreseen* as either certain or probable, but *not willed* as either means or end?
b. What is the objective good or evil of each unintended side effect?
c. What is the certitude or probability of each effect?
d. What is the urgency of the goods involved?
e. How great is the influence of the intended act and its intended effects?

Decision 2.
a. If there is no proportionate reason for willing a minor evil, or no proportionate reason for risking or permitting a major

evil, the analysis stops at this point. You are dealing with an unethical act.

    b. If there is a proportionate reason in the abstract, go to stage three.

Stage 3.   a. Is there an equally good method of attaining the good with less evil or risk of evil?

Decision 3.   a. If the answer to the above is yes, you should use the alternative, since you have no proportionate reason for the act you are considering.

    b. If the answer to the above question is no, you may act, since you have a proportionate reason for permitting or risking an evil in the concrete as well as in the abstract.

ANALYSIS OF THE XYZ CASE

Stage 1.   a. The directors wish to market a new product in order to keep the company in existence and to maintain their own control of it. They intend to put a small label on their product as a means of reducing the risk of its use by pregnant women.

    b. Everything willed is good. We may go on to stage two.

Stage 2.   a. If the directors succeed they will maintain the jobs of some five hundred workers. They are taking a risk of pregnant women using the drug and giving birth to deformed children.

    b. The first effect is good and a major one for the workers. The second effect is a major evil for both the mothers and the unborn children.

    c. It is impossible to calculate the probability of the good effect on the basis of the data given. This is a frequent occurrence in ethics. The evil effect will certainly follow for *some* women since people are careless about labels. We do not know how many women will be involved.

d. The need to keep the company in existence is urgent because of its financial condition. However, since people must rely on the company for information and protection from serious harm, the need of the mothers and the unborn children is equally if not more urgent.

e. The fact that the company markets the drugs directly to users makes it a major influence. However, the carelessness of people in reading labels means that the company is not the sole cause of the risk and the ultimate harm.

Decision 2.

a. The author feels that the company has no proportionate reason for taking the great risk involved since its warnings and controls are not adequate. If the drug were prescribed only by physicians who had been adequately warned and if the bottle contained prominent warnings, the harm would flow almost entirely from others so that the company could have a proportionate reason after doing everything possible to reduce risk.

b. Supposing that the company had tried everything to reduce risk, let us go on to stage three.

Stage 3.

a. The company could be kept in existence by merging with the larger company. The existence of this alternative would reduce the proportionality. If the company had not done everything to reduce risk, the existence of the alternative would reinforce the conclusion that it would be unethical to take the risk. The desire to maintain control of the company would have little weight in such an analysis.

Decision 3.   a. If the company cannot give adequate warnings and use effective controls, the existence of an alternate way of preserving the company and the jobs of employees would make it obligatory to merge.

In a case of this type, there is often room for disagreement as to the weights to be given to various factors. However, if the method is followed carefully, the businessman can at least be sure that he has made an honest attempt to act ethically. One can demand little more in human affairs where risk and uncertainty are a part of the fabric of life.

2

Economic
and Political Considerations

INTRODUCTION

The principles developed in the previous chapter apply to all men and all human actions. The businessman, however, is not only a man and a citizen but a manager of a group with a specific purpose. As a result, he has obligations which arise specifically his role as businessman. Since these obligations are additions to his basic duties, they form the proper matter of business ethics. In theory, the specifically business obligations can be derived by applying basic principles to particular business situations. In practice, the beginner is unable to do this effectively, since he is liable to overlook important factors.

The present chapter, then, introduces some general considerations about the economic and political functions of managers.[1] These considerations are necessary for the proper application of

[1] In addition to the books cited in later notes, the reader may want to consult Kenneth Boulding, *The Organizational Revolution* (New York, Harper & Row, 1953); Richard Eells, *The Meaning of Modern Business* (New York, Columbia University Press, 1960); Richard Eells and Clarence Walton, *Conceptual Foundations of Modern Business* (Homewood, Illinois, Irwin, 1961); Andrew Hacker, ed., *The Corporation Take-Over* (New York, Harper & Row, 1964); Edward S. Mason, ed., *The Corporation in Modern Society* (Cambridge, Massachusetts, Harvard University Press, 1959); Charles E. Summer and Jeremiah J. O'Connell, *The Managerial Mind* (Homewood, Illinois, Irwin, 1964).

principles to the myriad problems which occupy the remainder of this book. While the relative importance of these factors varies with the size of the firm and its position to the economy as a whole, they are involved in nearly all business situations.

THE PURPOSE OF THE FIRM

From the *social point* of view, firms exist to supply goods and services to consumers as efficiently as possible. From the *individual point of view*, the firm exists to supply income, power, prestige, creative satisfaction, or a combination of these to those who work for or with it. To put it another way, the manager is obliged to run the firm as efficiently as possible within the limits set by the basic ethics presented in the previous chapter. This is not an easy task, for the two sets of goals are intertwined in such a way that the neglect of any one can destroy or injure the others. In short, the manager must reconcile claims and harmonize means so that all legitimate goals are obtained by ethical means.

To the extent that the manager realizes the social goal of efficient production of goods and services designed to satisfy human needs and desires for useful goods, he should show a profit. Profits, though they motivate some individuals, are not the goal of the firm itself so much as a *possible* measure of its performance. The word *possible* in the previous sentence is important, for a profit can result from luck, fraud, coercion, or from exploitation of ignorance and irrationality, as well as from economic efficiency. Profits, in brief, are ambiguous both ethically and economically. For this reason, we prefer to say that the manager businessman is obliged to be efficient rather than obliged to make a profit.

The necessity and hence the obligatory character of human economic efficiency needs to be stressed. On it depends not only the survival of the firm but the livelihood of employees, owners and managers. Moreover, the ability of people to satisfy needs and useful desires depends on efficiency so long as even some means are scarce. This very pragmatic approach should not shock anyone, providing the idea of human economic efficiency is not narrowed artificially. Efficient management demands long-run as well as short-run maximization. It stresses careful use of physical resources, worker morale, executive development, research, and good relations with the community and the society at large. Each one of these factors is a means to the end which cannot be neglected if the firm is to do its job. Each one of these factors also has impacts on human beings which cannot be disregarded, since the manager of a firm is a man who must respect the dignity of others. What must be stressed is the fact that the firm is not a philanthropic or charitable institution. It is a tool, a group organized to serve a very specific end, and its purpose cannot be disregarded without great harm to society and individuals.

It should be noted that the specific purpose of a firm or corporation is not inalterable. Eells' *The Government of Corporations,* and Berle's *The American Republic*[2] study the growing demands being made on business and show the directions in which the corporation may have to move if it is to survive. In Chapter Fourteen, we shall return to some of the problems involved in determining what the corporation must do and be tomorrow. For the present, we shall content ourselves with a simple and manageable concept of efficiency in the production and distribution of economic goods and services in a market economy.

THE SOCIETAL NATURE OF THE FIRM

If the firm is to attain its end and realize its goals, all people involved must cooperate. In short, a firm is a society which cannot realize its purposes without human cooperation and a unity of purpose. In the firm as elsewhere, this cooperation is not automatic, but is created by managers. It is for this reason that managers have to plan, organize, and control the activities of men so that the firm will prosper. This means that the manager fulfills his obligations to individuals largely by fulfilling his obligations to the firm. He is not free to subordinate the good of the firm to one or two individuals since this harms dozens, hundreds, even hundreds of thousands who depend on the firm for their livelihood and need-satisfaction.

[2] Richard Eells, *The Government of Corporations* (New York, Free Press, 1962); Adolph A. Berle, *The American Economic Republic* (New York, Harcourt, Brace & World, 1963).

In political terminology, the manager is an authority who is in charge of the public good and social weal of a firm. This good is as dependent on the contributions of members as the members are dependent on the distribution of the goods of the firm. The social good of the firm, however, is not identical with the good of the members.[3] This social good is composed of various factors which have the following characteristics.

1. They are produced by the cooperation of many people.
2. They belong to the firm and not to any member no matter what the law may say.
3. All members benefit in some way from the existence of these factors.

Thus, the social good of a firm comprises not only physical equipment, patents, and contracts, but good will, morale, loyalty, the unity of the managerial team, and its reputation. The manager is in charge of producing and combining these factors so that the firm can attain its goal. To the extent that he succeeds, he will provide contributors and workers with income and other satisfactions. If he fails, both consumers and employees suffer. Even if stockholders own the company, in the sense that they have a right to a share in the liquidation, it should be clear that they do not own the social good, since most of it would disappear in a liquidation. For all practical purposes, stockholders are most accurately treated as remote contributors rather than as owners. We shall return to this point in Chapter Twelve when treating the firm's relationships with stockholders.

THE RIGHTS AND OBLIGATIONS OF MANAGEMENT

The obligation to manage the firm gives rise to the right to manage. To put it another way, the basic authority of the manager arises from his function. This is true even in the case where the manager is the sole owner. His property right may give

---

[3] This view of the public or common good is well developed by Thomas E. Davitt, S.J., in *Elements of Law* (Boston, Little, Brown, 1959). Real insight can be gained by reading Yves R. Simon, *Philosophy of Democratic Government* (Chicago, University of Chicago Press, Phoenix Books, 1951), pp. 1-71.

him control over various things, but it does not give him authority over workers, their time and energies. He obtains this latter right by means of the work contract which binds the employee to cooperate for the good of the firm in return for definite benefits.

While the work contract is the source of most managerial authority, it is unfortunately so vague that it can and does give rise to many disputes concerning the exact limits of management rights. In an age when employers had the power to enforce nearly all of their desires, it was assumed that management had all rights not explicitly denied by law or the work contract. In the day of unions, however, it is assumed that management has only such rights as are explicitly given it by formal agreement. In short, newer thinkers would claim that management operates on the basis of rights delegated either by the owners or by the workers. Moreover, in this view of things, management is not the sole interpreter of the terms of the delegation.

Although this question is of the utmost importance, it cannot be fully developed in a short book. For the present then, we will discuss certain limits on management authority, and consider practical suggestions for the removal of gray areas.

In the first place, management authority is certainly limited by its purpose—the good of the firm. A manager does not have the right to use the firm as a personal toy. Even though he has the *power* to subordinate the good of the firm to his own personal profit or whim, he does not have the *right* or authority to do so. This limitation can be applied to cases concerning the use of insider information and to conflict of interest cases as well as to the area involved with executive compensations, stock options, and expansion plans.

In the second place, management authority is limited by the clear rights of workers, stockholders, suppliers, dealers, and the community at large. Since most of these rights are relative, the line is not always clear, but it is there somewhere under the smoke and haze. As a result, the ethical manager must constantly be asking himself if his act is a reasonable interference with another's search for even useful goods. The employer, for example, should look long and hard at orders or policies which interfere with the home life of employees, their political activity, personal privacy, and freedom to change jobs.

A manager may limit relative freedom for reasonable cause related to the good of the firm, but it is not always easy to decide what is reasonable. Moreover, since we tend to exaggerate our own interests and minimize those of other men, correctives are needed. A free contract which specifies and limits can be a useful aid in this area. A contract, however, really helps only if it is free and not the result of power positions, fraud, and ignorance. Custom too may be a guide to what is reasonable and unreasonable, but it is not decisive since conditions change and demand the readjustment of both contracts and customs.

While there are many undefined areas where there is no clear objective demarcation between the rights of management and the rights of other groups, this does not automatically give management the right to make unilateral decisions which can change the work contract by interpretation. This can be seen by comparing the management process to the legislative process in the political order. There are differences between them, but the similarities are great enough to be significant

In the political order, experience has shown us that unilateral decisions by power holders constitute a threat to individual rights and freedom. As a result, power has been institutionalized by a constitution which provides for due process and a system of checks and balances. Thus, the legislator is supposed to hear all points of view; the executive must answer to the courts; and the courts must observe procedures designed to reduce arbitrary decisions. Behind our political institutions is the realization that rights and obligations cannot be unilaterally determined, but must reflect the various interests involved. Those who created our judicial system also recognized that the arbitrary application of even a basically just law may lead to injustice in the long run.

I suspect that, in the business world, much of the dispute about management rights is really a dispute about the way in which decisions are made and enforced rather than about the right of management to make them. In short, there is a suspicion that what people fear is not management authority but management power which is not checked by an institutional framework providing for both bilateral decisions and due process. The problem cannot be solved without some form of corporate constitutionalism.

No matter what stand one takes in theory, in practice sound

management would demand that attention be given to the reasoned opinions of those affected as well as to the development of a system which removes suspicion of arbitrary application. Much of this already exists in the area of collective bargaining, but as we shall see in later chapters, much remains to be done to insure justice on the management level itself.

Much of this may sound foreign to the ears of the rugged individualist, but he should be realistic enough to see that one rules only by the consent of the governed. If that consent is extorted or forced, we are dealing with tyranny, whether in a nation or a corporation. The manager is also sitting on a powder keg when there is no real assent to his authority. On the other hand, when the consent is freely given and the work contract mutually acceptable, a climate will exist in which trust and mutual confidence reinforce productivity as well as fair dealing.[4]

THE FIRM AND ITS ECONOMIC RELATIONSHIPS

The businessman's rights are limited not only by the rights of his own employees, but by those of the various groups with whom he must deal. Thus, he must consider the impact of his decisions on stockholders, suppliers, dealers, competitors, customers, unions, local communities, and on the economic system as a whole. This is merely to say that the firm is part of a total economic and political system and not an island without foreign relations. Like employees, the economic groups that deal with or are affected by the firm have rights which must be respected.

The rights and legitimate claims of the various groups connected with or related to the firm are not always clear. The manager, indeed, must mediate between these claims, seek to reconcile them and to maximize the good of the firm and the system of which it is a part. This is not merely a question of justice but of business efficiency, since the firm cannot long exist without the continued co-

---

[4] The reader is referred to the thesis of Douglas McGregor in *The Human Side of Enterprise* (New York, McGraw-Hill, 1960). For a stimulating commentary on the importance of attitudes and values, see Charles D. Flory, ed., *Managers for Tomorrow* (New York, NAL World Literature, 1965).

operation of all these groups. Sometimes a firm can exploit another group, but in the long run the good of the firm is bound up with the interests of all its claimants.

While it may not be easy to determine what is fair in each and every case, the manager must realize that power, fraud, ignorance, and passion can vitiate the relationships of justice and even destroy the system of exchange and cooperation. He must, then, continually distinguish between what he can do because of his power, and what is fair when all factors have been considered. This, after all, is the meaning of responsible self-regulation.

BUSINESS POWER AND THE BROADER SOCIETY

The problem of power and the limits of authority within the firm bring us to the relationship between the firm and the broader society. While this topic will be discussed in greater detail toward the end of the volume, certain remarks should be made here and now in order to provide at least a framework for discussion. This is particularly important, for some readers might think that the ethics of the firm involve only individuals and economic groups such as stockholders, suppliers, dealers, and competitors.

In classic economic theory, the optimum relationship between a firm and the good of the whole society was supposed to be established automatically. As a result, businessmen did not have to worry about broad social impacts. The classical theory, however, rested on assumptions which are no longer true, if they ever were. The modern businessman must face problems of national policy if he is to fulfill his duties as a citizen. It is not easy to delineate these duties or to assign precise responsibilities, but there can be little doubt that they do exist.

In line with the principles governing proportionality, the businessman must certainly seek to minimize the harmful impacts of his activities. Realistically, however, he is often not in a position to do this except by entering into cooperative arrangements with the industry, the unions, and the government. As a result, many of the businessman's obligations in this area are really transformed into a general obligation to work with others for the betterment of society. This, as we shall see time and time again, means that he must accept his responsibility as a citizen and transcend the *status quo* and the accepted practices of business in the past. It does not mean that he must become a social reformer on a large scale or turn his business into a benevolent association. Neither activity would really serve society in the long run.

In order to arrive at a new perspective on his relation to the broader society, the business must consider some of the facts of life which differentiate business today from business a hundred years ago. The principal fact is that of power and of society's attitude toward it.

No society can be indifferent either to the fact of power or to the way in which it is used. It must be concerned not only with actual misuses of power but with potential misuses as well. There are several reasons for this. In the first place, power is not ethically neutral. Secondly, power must be made to serve society and all men. Finally, the protection of rights involves control of the power to abuse rights.

Power is not ethically neutral, even though it is often said that we may judge it by its uses and the techniques used to generate it. Certainly, the uses and methods of generating power have ethical significance, but so does the fact of power itself. To put it another way, ethics is concerned not only with intentions and the foreseen effects of power, but also with its inherent tendencies which may not be recognized by those who wield power.

Lord Acton felt that power corrupts and that absolute power corrupts absolutely. While this may be an overly pessimistic view of the inherent tendencies of power, the statement contains a great deal of truth. It is a truth which has been confirmed by the lessons of history and considered by the framers of the American Constitution who designed a system of checks and balances. We do not know exactly how power corrupts, but it seems to intoxicate and convince men that its mere possession justifies their acts and frees them from the ethics of the weak and powerless.

It should be noted that the dangers inherent in power apply to government power as well as private power, to union power as well as to business power. As a result, there is need for a continual re-evaluation of all institutions designed to control power in a society. Just as we examine the functioning of our political machinery to see if it serves the people, we must examine our economic system with the same end in view. Without constant surveillance and scrutiny, there is no guaranteed way to preserve freedom, protect rights, and direct the forces of society to worthy goals. Slogans will not do the job, nor will power struggles designed to advance the interest of one group at the expense of another.

In our present American situation, business must admit that it has great power which is less than perfectly channeled in its responses to the needs of society. Sometimes this power is gained because the business community faces unorganized and uninformed consumers. Sometimes it exists because the lobbies and the public relations department of business are better equipped to influence legislation than is the general public which is so often inarticulate and ignorant. Possibly the greatest source of power lies in the pooled intelligence and resources of the business community. No matter what the source of the power, society cannot be indifferent to either its actual or potential uses. It follows that businessmen must also be interested in these questions if they are to be good citizens as well as efficient handlers of the society's resources.

Because this is a book for beginners, limited space is given to the consideration of these vital social questions. They exist, however, and must be answered if the nation and the business community are to prosper.

THE HIERARCHY OF GOALS

The previous pages place the manager, whether he be an owner or an agent, at the center of a network of relationships to persons, groups, and things. By the very nature of his jobs, he must, for both business and ethical reasons, consider the impact of his actions on all to which he is related. He must seek to reconcile claims within a framework that recognizes the rights and needs of both individuals and groups. This is a very large order. It cannot be filled unless the manager has real technical competence and a well thought out hierarchy of goals.

There is no ready-made formula which gives each goal a precise place in relation to the dignity of the human person. The golden rule may help to form sound ethical attitudes, but it cannot be applied without recognizing the demands of concrete situations. What is a just decision today may be an unjust decision tomorrow if key conditions have changed. A goal which must take a high place today may have to be subordinated tomorrow. At best, then, only some general considerations can be given. The manager can use these in applying the methods of the first chapter to the problems he meets in business.

The quasi-absolute rights of real persons take precedence over the claims of either the company or the general society. This is to say that the person as such may never be directly and deliberately subordinated to the good of any group. The reason is clear. Groups exist to help individuals and cannot justify deliberately willing the destruction of the person. Fortunately, the temptation to use a man as a mere thing is fairly rare in modern business, so this first rule of precedence should not have to be invoked too often.

This should not cause us to overlook the fact that this rule of precedence can be violated. The firm which forces an employee to act against his conscience is subordinating an absolute and inalienable right of a person to the company. The companies which once worked men six days a week, ten hours a day, in deep mines certainly subordinated the person to the company in effect, if not in intent. Perhaps workers had proportionate reasons for taking such risks, but it is difficult to see how the companies did. Although a man may not be used as a means that is directly and deliberately subordinated to the company, there can be and are sufficient reasons for asking a worker to freely risk even his life once all precautions have been taken. The work of high steel erectors and sand hogs is inherently dangerous, but it is not necessarily unethical to hire men for such jobs.

Conflicts about relative rights can be settled in favor of a party whose rights are clearly spelled out in a contract. Where there is no such contract or where the contract is not a truly free agreement, the dispute can often be resolved by examining the reasonably founded expectations of the parties involved. Where neither policy, custom, nor accepted practice gives a clue to what is a reasonable expectation, fairness seems to demand that either collective bargaining or outside arbitration be used lest selfishness dominate.

By contract the claims of workers to their wages takes precedence over the manager's desire to expand. By custom, if not by law, the need of the firm to expand will take precedence over the claims of stockholders to a dividend. There are, however, no rules for deciding whether the demand of workers for a wage increase over a fair wage will take precedence over the claims of stockholders.[5] It is for this reason that bargaining and arbitration are necessary lest the issue be settled by power alone. On the other hand, in a conflict between the workers' need for wages which are decent and the stockholders' desire for a dividend, the worker would take precedence. Wages are the basic income for workers, while dividends are generally only relative goods for most stockholders. In theory too, stockholders have agreed to take risks, while workers have not.

The needs of the nation take precedence over the needs of the firm, but what is merely useful for the nation does not take precedence over what is necessary for the functioning of the firm. Ultimately, the decisions in this area of conflict have to be made by the government, but the rule can guide the businessman in his attitude toward the passage of new laws.

All of this comes down to saying that the application of the analysis given at the end of Chapter One is more complicated than it might seem. This should surprise no one who understands management, for the function is complicated by its nature. This complexity, however, may help to explain why outsiders fail to realize the true problems of the businessman and why insiders are often afraid to face the true challenge of business ethics.

Ethics is necessary, but it is not sufficient to insure justice in societies, whether they be corporations or political entities. There are many areas of life and business where there are no ready-made answers. Often, fairness will depend on the existence of free contracts which create order where none existed before. Free contracts in their turn need the support of society and law which prevents one party from dominating another. In addition, there are other areas where so many people have an interest that fairness demands that all parties be represented and that society itself assign obligations and draw up rules to establish order where none exists by the nature of the case. Ethics can help in providing general guide lines, but it is no substitute for that creative decision-making which is an essential

[5] On this point, see Benjamin L. Masse, S.J., *Justice for All* (Milwaukee, Bruce, 1964), pp. 50-52.

function of human social life. No one should be disappointed if ethics often points up problems without being able to give a definitive solution.

These last remarks should serve to reinforce the importance of social institutions which protect rights and enable men to realize their potential. Good will and an enlightened conscience are not enough unless they can be expressed in effective institutions. We may say that there is a general obligation to work for the creation of such systems and rules as will promote the specifically human end of which we spoke in Chapter One. It is for this reason that the truly ethical man will give full consideration to the harmful effects of his acts upon society and to the need for perfecting the society itself.

II

Relationship of
the Firm to the Employee

3

Hiring and Firing

INTRODUCTION

The ethics of hiring and firing are governed by the dignity of the applicant or worker, by the contractual relation between employer and employee, and by the purpose of the firm. The personnel manager and policy makers must guard against discrimination, breach of contract, and decisions which are not conducive to efficiency and worker morale.

As a general rule, the firm hires men in order to increase its production and productivity. Family companies may want to supply jobs to relatives, but even here the efficiency of the operation must be considered lest the firm, its employees, and the general public suffer harm. The ethics of hiring is largely governed by the norm of efficiency as it was outlined in Chapter Two. A man is hired for the benefit of the firm and should be selected on the basis of his ability and willingness to serve the social good of the company and the public.

The manager who hires the best people available within the limits set by his salary scale and recruiting budget is acting ethically. If he discriminates between applicants it must be on the basis of job-related qualifications. This obligation arises not only from his basic duty to the firm, but from his obligation to treat people equally in those areas where they are equal. To act on caprice or prejudice is to act irrationally and unethically. In short, selection on the basis of factors which are not job-related is both an insult to human dignity and a failure to serve the firm.

These basic duties have been written in the Civil Rights Act of 1964.[1] The law admits that religon, sex, and national origin can be *bona fide* job qualifications in some special and carefully defined situations. Race and color, however, are never admitted as job qualifications. There might be a special case where race and color could have something to do with job performance, but in general the law is sound.

The law extends the area of ethical obligation, for it excludes some of the ethical exceptions which could otherwise provide temporary excuses. In the absence of the law, for example, a man might hesitate in hiring a Negro because he anticipated serious trouble from his prejudiced employees. Today such a fear does not excuse employers affected by the law. Others must make sure their fear is well grounded before they can invoke the prejudices of third parties as a temporary excuse for discrimination in hiring practices.

DETERMINING JOB QUALIFICATIONS

Both ethics and the law demand that managers define concrete *bona fide* job qualifications. This is a difficult task, but a necessary one. It involves the suitability of the applicant for the immediate job and his ability to profit from training for more important positions. Considering the cost of hiring and training workers, the potential for advancement is certainly a *bona fide* employment qualification.

When job qualifications have been determined, the manager must apply his policy intelligently. He must decide on the combination of interviews and tests and check their predictive value. While the law permits the use of professionally developed tests if there is no intention of discriminating unfairly, the conscientious

[1] For text and clear analysis, see "Civil Rights Act of 1964," *NAM Law Department Reviews* (Washington, D.C., National Association of Manufacturers, July, 1964). For more detailed information on the problems involved, see Charles A. Kothe, *A Tale of 22 Cities: Report on Title VII of the Civil Rights Act of 1964* (Washington, D.C., National Association of Manufacturers, 1965); and George F. Doriot, ed., *The Management of Racial Integration in Business* (New York, McGraw-Hill, 1965).

employer will recognize that pencil-and-paper tests may discriminate against culturally deprived groups.[2] This will not necessarily be unethical discrimination. If the job demands skill in reading, writing and arithmetic, it is certainly not discriminatory to use professionally developed pencil-and-paper tests. On the other hand, if neither the immediate job nor the training for future jobs demands such skills, the tests could be unfair in effect if not in intent. Similarly, the pertinence of vocabulary level, cultural knowledge, and the like are to be judged in terms of the jobs to be filled.

The problem is relatively simple in screening applicants for ordinary industrial jobs. Unfortunately, jobs that involve the handling of people demand qualifications that are intangible and cannot be revealed by standardized tests. General culture, voice, diction, poise, and the ability to socialize are all relevant to a great many jobs, yet they are subject to considerable vagueness of definition. Even when such factors are not decisive, they are important plus values. In some cases, the factors are so important that companies will spend time and money entertaining not only the applicant but his wife to discover their suitability to the company. The use of such criteria is ethical if there is no discrimination based on qualifications unrelated to the job.

THE USE OF STATISTICS

Many tests are based on statistical probability. When one is dealing with groups, the use of statistics is certainly justified, since they have been developed from and for groups. A man is justified in not locating his plant in an area where statistical studies show the average productivity is low. While there may be many good workers in the area, his decision is concerned with the group and not with individuals.

In the hiring situation, we are dealing with individuals and not with groups; statistical data must be put aside while we investigate the individual. The fact that sixty percent of the people in a given

[2] There will be many problems of interpretation in this area, but the issue will always be whether or not the discrimination is relevant to job qualifications. Employers, however, should watch court decisions carefully, since early rulings in the Motorola case give the impression that some might interpret any discrimination as illegal even though job-related.

group suffer from eye strain does not tell me anything about the individual before me. As a result, I would be unjust in attributing to him the statistical characteristics of the group to which he belongs. Something similar may be said when we are dealing not with careful, scientific studies but with our own ideas about groups. Perhaps sixty percent of the teen-agers I know personally are extroverts, but even if my impression is correct, it does not tell me anything about this particular teen-ager. Individuals are always to be treated as individuals.

PREFERENTIAL HIRING

In the present emotionally charged atmosphere, many individuals claim that companies should engage in preferential hiring of Negroes and other minority groups. They reason that a company has an obligation to make restitution for the sins of the past. In addition, they say that such hiring alone can help us to solve our national problem.

While these arguments have a plausible ring to them, they rest on a dubious foundation and contradict basic ethical principles. In the first place, membership in a group should neither help nor hinder a man unless it is relevant to the purpose or reasonable conditions of hiring. Secondly, although society as a whole may have an obligation to help disadvantaged citizens, it must respect the rights of others and the demands of the common good itself. In any event, the help would have to be based on need rather than on some factor such as color which has only an accidental connection with need. Thirdly, it is difficult to see how an individual living today can be made responsible for the acts of an individual long since dead. It is even more difficult to see how the sin of my grandfather against an individual gives me an obligation toward the grandson of that individual unless I am unjustly in possession of property which he should have inherited. Society has obligations, and I as a citizen may have an obligation to cooperate with society. However, this obligation is based on an awareness of present need and not on a theory of inherited guilt.

It is wrong to exclude a man because he is a Negro. It is equally wrong to exclude him because he is not a Negro. Furthermore, most of our Civil Rights legislation, especially on the state level, would appear to forbid such practices. Not only ethics and law, but good business forbids preferential hiring. Much of the opposition to integration and fair employment practices springs from the fear that Negroes will reduce the number of jobs available to other races. Preferential hiring can only increase those fears by providing an objective basis for the anxiety. This can only make it more difficult to integrate work forces at the same time that it weakens morale.

No one will deny that the installation of fair hiring practices will cause difficulties in some plants and in some sections of the country. Human nature and its deep-rooted prejudices are not easily changed even with the aid of the law. Despite this, men do have a sense of fairness which can be developed if management prepares the way and establishes its own reputation for justice. The difficulties should be considered a challenge to management skills rather than an excuse for either inaction or imprudent crusading.

Our firm stand against preferential hiring by companies is not a stand against government and industry programs designed to help *all* the disadvantaged help themselves. Retraining programs and even training programs designed to upgrade job qualifications are certainly in order when they are *available to all* in need regardless of the person's race, color, creed, sex, religion, and national origin. This does not presuppose any theory of collective guilt, but merely implies that society has an obligation to help its present citizens help themselves.

In addition to training programs open to all, companies can often profitably recruit employees from schools and areas where Negroes and other disadvantaged groups predominate. Such procedures are not preferential; they are creative extensions of job opportunities. While there may be no strict duty to do these things, progressive management should not overlook the potential contribution of highly motivated applicants whose talents have long been wasted.[3]

[3] Theodore V. Purcell, S.J., "Management Versus Jim Crow," *Management of Personnel Quarterly*, Vol. 1 (Summer, 1962), p. 2, notes that in a study of one industry the Negro women workers were the best educated, but had been kept doing routine assembly-line jobs. This is typical of the waste discrimination causes.

NEPOTISM

Nepotism is potentially a case of preferential hiring. It may, however, have a legitimate place in the family firm where the hiring looks not only to efficiency, but to providing jobs for relatives. In these cases, the preference can be justified to a certain extent by the peculiar purpose of the firm. In all other cases, nepotism is unethical only if it involves real favoritism or discrimination.

In the *Harvard Business Review*,[4] the respondents to a questionnaire indicated that despite some disagreements, businessmen are concerned with the qualifications and impact of the relative. Assuming that the relative has qualifications at least roughly equal to other candidates, the decision should be based on a realistic evaluation of the effect of this hiring on the firm. The businessman must ask himself questions like the following: Would hiring this man create jealousy and resentment? Will it discourage qualified outsiders from seeking work with the company? Will it create problems in firing and demoting? Will it inhibit the relative's development? Will it cause problems inside the family? It should be remembered that, in itself, being a relative is neither a virtue or a vice. Ethically then, decisions should be made with a consideration of the potential impacts of the hiring decision as well as on the basis of the candidate's qualifications.

SPECIAL PROBLEMS

In theory, fair employment practices should pose no problems to the capable businessman. In practice, he may face real difficulties. Hiring hall procedures by unions who do not obey the law, discrimination by employment agencies, moral and economic pressures from friends, associates, and customers may entangle the businessman. While we cannot discuss all of these problems in detail, the following points should be kept in mind. If the employer has no intention of discriminating and is not covered by the law, he may

[4] David W. Ewing, "Is Nepotism So Bad?," *Harvard Business Review*, Vol. 43 (January-February, 1965), pp. 22 ff.

often have a proportionate reason for cooperating with those who discriminate. Fear and timidity, however, are not permanent excuses. Indeed, the very difficulties which create a temporary excuse give rise to an obligation to remedy the factors which create the problem. In the concrete, this may mean working for the passage of laws which will enable men of good will to do the right thing without undue hardship. In other cases, it may involve cooperation with community groups attempting to eliminate prejudice. When possible, it will involve circumventing unions, hiring halls, and employment agencies which do discriminate.

We must stress the fact that since many problems cannot be solved by isolated individuals or by businessmen alone, there is an obligation to enter into broader forms of social cooperation. Ending discrimination in hiring helps to equalize opportunity, but it does not do away with the unnatural inequalities arising from poor education and poor family background. This residual but huge inequality is not solely or specially the problem of business, but it cannot be solved without the help of business. Therefore, business must at least support if not initiate programs designed to attack the root problems.

PROMOTIONS

The same principles apply to both hiring and promotions. In brief, job qualifications should dominate all decisions in the vast majority of cases. Unfortunately, the existence of demands for the recognition of seniority complicates this question.

Seniority *of itself* is no index of competence. It is not even an index of loyalty since it may result from laziness or cowardice. In the abstract, then, seniority has no bearing on a decision to promote. In the concrete, seniority may indicate real job qualifications as well as length of service. Moreover, the expectations of workers, whether reasonable or not, may change the significance of seniority.[5] If workers expect seniority to count, management's disregard of their opinion may injure morale. On the other hand, if too much attention is

[5] Philip Selznick and Howard Vollmer, *Rule of Law in Industry: Seniority Rights* (Berkeley, California, Institute of Industrial Relations, 1962), suggests that these exectations may not be what they appear to be.

given to mere years of service, management may discourage real initiative and lose talented young workers and executives.

Similar problems beset the manager who must decide whether to promote from within or to go outside the company. In the abstract, he should look only to competence. In the concrete, he must consider the impact of his decision on his employees, whether or not their attitudes are unreasonable. Here, as elsewhere, the existence of carefully written and fully promulgated policies can do much to control expectations and make sound ethical and business decisions easier to execute.

Some of the most difficult problems arise when a man has been promoted to a job which he cannot handle or which will seriously harm his health. Demoting such an individual not only involves wounding his pride and reducing his income, but also makes a public admission of management failure. On the other hand, if the situation is allowed to continue, the man's assistants and the company will suffer harm.

Generally such problems are unpleasant to meet head-on. As a result, management attempts to evolve ingenious compromises. Sometimes, the man is given an assistant or moved horizontally to a job he can handle. Sometimes job assignments are changed so that the work load or type of work is different. Such manoeuvres are possible in large or very profitable companies, but may be too expensive in others. In these circumstances, it is generally necessary to seek a tactful method of demotion which frequently turns out to be better for the man involved as for all others.

Nearly all our remarks on special problems and promotions indicate that the primacy of job qualifications is not absolute. A company is composed of men, not cyphers, so that the principle has to be adjusted to the concrete possibilities. What must be avoided is the arbitrary disregard of principle or the acceptance of unjust situations as immutable.

FIRING

In the absence of an explicit work contract, it was formerly assumed that both employer and employee had a right to terminate their agreement at will. Some individuals still assume this to be true. Quite aside from legal provisions, however, there are implicit contracts which limit or modify the right of both employer and employee. In many countries these modifications have become the subject of law.[6] In the United States, they are often stated in collective bargaining agreements as well as in labor law. As we shall see later, good business ethics probably demands the extension of both the law and explicit contractual provisions. First, we shall take a look at the basic ethics involved.

Regardless of explicit contractual provisions, both employer and employee have obligations to each other which arise first from their common humanity and secondly from the definite social situation in which their agreement was made. This means that each side must take into consideration the legitimate interests and expectations of the other. While such interests may not always be decisive, they must be considered lest one be indifferent to the good of another human being.

The employer's obligations fall into three headings.
1. He must dismiss only for just cause.
2. He must observe due process.
3. He must seek to mitigate the harmful effects of dismissal, due attention being given to proportionality.

JUST CAUSE

Although the phrase "just cause" is necessarily vague, it certainly includes only factors pertinent to the running of a business. Thus the whim of the employer, his personal political convictions, and the annoying mannerisms of an employee are not just causes. Just causes will include mechanization, reduction in output, violation of discipline including conduct harmful to other workers, negligence, old age, frequent illness, and prolonged absenteeism which is harmful to either the business or other workers.

It should be noted that an employer not only may dismiss for such just causes, but often *must* do so. While our emotions may balk at dismissing a poor employee who has a large number of children, this act may be necessary to protect the company and/or other

[6] For a brief summary, read International Labour Conference, Forty-Sixth Session, *Termination of Employment* (Geneva, International Labour Office, 1962.)

workers. The lazy worker, for example, not only robs the business of the purchased services, but demoralizes others and reduces overall efficiency. The dishonest worker harms the firm not only by his own thefts, but by inducing others to follow his example. For these reasons, sentiment must give way to an objective evaluation of the situation.

In many cases sentiment harms not only the firm but the worker who should be fired. Tacit consent to inefficiency, laziness or dishonesty only reinforces bad habits and makes it harder and harder to reform. Moreover, tacit consent can fill in the details in the work contract and set up false if powerful expectations which render dismissal progressively more difficult.

Since length of service changes the relationship and so the implicit contract, the reason for dismissal must be more serious in the case of a veteran employee than in the case of an apprentice. There are several reasons for this. The efficiency of a business depends, in the vast majority of cases, on the stability of its work force. As a result, anything which disturbs confidence in the employer's recognition of service is liable to have harmful effects on both morale and recruiting. Simple common sense then would indicate that the reason for dismissal must offset this risk. In addition, senior employees have often sacrificed opportunities in order to stay with a company.

Carefully drawn up company policy can help to remove arbitrariness and reduce dissatisfaction. Some companies, for example, will not dismiss a worker over fifty who has been with them at least twenty years except for the grossest negligence or incapacity. Others provide for shifting burdens from older workers and putting them where they can pass on experience even though they may not be able to meet full job requirements.

DUE PROCESS

Due process safeguards not only the rights of the employee but the morale of other workers. It is not enough to be just. One must also appear just if the potentially harmful effects of dismissal are to be mitigated. Due process gives the assurance that decisions are not made arbitrarily and thus reinforces the confidence of the work force. Furthermore, because due process involves a system of checks and balances, it increases the objectivity of decisions.

The need for objectivity should be apparent. For many employers, dismissals are a highly emotional subject. All too often employers are so concerned with a small set of factors that they lose the overall view necessary for making decisions which are ethically and economically sound. For example, the fact that an incapable employee has a large family and long years of service does not generally offset such evils as demoralization of the work force and serious inefficiency. To put it another way, the employer must remember that he has an obligation to protect all of his workers and the interest of customers and owners. As a result, he needs some method of assuring adequate consideration of all of the factors involved. Ethically he should always use the sanctions which cause the least harm, but he should not lose sight of the fact that when warnings have been given, firing may be the only means left.

The exact process to be used cannot be determined in the abstract. Elaborate measures will be both unnecessary and too costly for the small firm while overly simple procedures may be useless in a large one. In general, however, a workable procedure will be the result of an agreement worked out between management and employees.

MITIGATION OF HARMFUL EFFECTS

Even though an employer is justified in firing a worker, he must seek to mitigate the harmful effects of dismissal. Although a man may have a proportionate reason for risking or permitting the harmful effects of a dismissal, he still has the basic obligation of using reasonable means to minimize the harm. This is recognized by ethical employers as well as by the law in many countries. In the United States, moreover, we have devised public means of lessening the effects of dismissal. The Unemployment Compensation Law is the principal example. However, since unemployment benefits are in many cases very meager, the employer may still have personal obligations.

Giving adequate notice of dismissal is one of the easier and more obvious methods of mitigating impacts. It costs the employer little and permits the employee to look for other work. Furthermore, it provides for some period of delay during which appeals can be made. It is difficult to determine the proper length of time of the notice period, but it would seem to be prudent for this to be stated explicitly in the work contract. Formal policy in these cases as in so many others regularizes expectations and so reinforces confidence in the fairness of the employer.

The obligation to mitigate harmful effects can be particularly serious in cases of plant relocation, major layoffs, and automation. The reason is simply that in these cases not only the workers and their families but tradesmen and, in some cases, entire communities may be affected. While it is impossible to specify which means of mitigation are to be used in a given case, there are many available. Adequate notice, retraining, and relocation of workers are possible procedures which may lessen harmful effects.

It should be recognized that in some cases the need for massive layoffs results from management's failure to do its job or from its refusal to find means of removing the underlying causes. For example, many businesses are highly seasonal, not because this is absolutely necessary, but because the employers have accepted a given situation as natural. Since it is good business as well as good ethics to iron out seasonal fluctuations, management should not overlook obligations in this area. Quite frequently the causes of seasonal variation can only be attacked by broad economic cooperation. While such cooperation may be foreign to the mentality of many businessmen, the fact remains that it can be necessary and therefore obligatory.

THE OBLIGATIONS OF EMPLOYEES

Although most obligations of the employee will be treated in Chapters Six, Seven and Eight, it should be noted that the implicit contract of employment binds both parties. Like the employer, the employee must make his decision with consideration for the welfare of the company and of his fellow workers. He may be free to quit at the end of his formal contract, but fair dealing requires that adequate notice be given in most cases. Indeed, unless there is a grounded fear of unjust retaliation, fairness would generally demand that employers be given a chance to match offers and to remedy causes of dissatisfaction. After all, the management too has its reasonably founded expectations.

SOME POINTS OF BROADER SIGNIFICANCE

In the previous pages we have had occasion to mention two points which will appear so frequently that they deserve to be underlined and explained lest their significance escape the reader. First, *carefully worked out policies can prevent many problems.* Secondly, *in many areas a policy should be the result of bilateral agreements if it is to be truly fair.*

A careful policy not only regularizes expectations but gives some assurance that decisions will not be made in an arbitrary manner. Good business alone would seem to demand such policy. Frequently, men confuse policy with detailed rule-making and avoid the task, since they think the situation too complex. Often, avoidance of the task actually results from the inability to deal with a problem or the unwillingness to limit the arbitrary. While there is some justification for moving slowly when the situation is complicated, a lack of executive talent and an insecure personality is betrayed by the failure to face problems and make commitments. These two characteristics plus the absence of policy can only breed ethical problems and cause worker dissatisfaction. Although many men will not recognize such attitudes as moral defects, experience shows that they generate as much unethical conduct as does downright dishonesty.

Our insistence on the need for bilateral agreements runs counter to the idea that management rights extend to everything that is not explicitly denied them by law or contract. While we do not intend to deny that management has and must have spheres of independent judgment, it should be recognized that men are rightfully less and less willing to enter into work contracts where one party lays down all conditions and reserves the right to interpret the contract. Resentment of such situations has promoted unionism and collective bargaining. While all problems may not be solved by collective agreements, since these too can be effected by power rather than by reasoned discourse, there is much to recommend them. Among other things men feel a greater obligation to abide by free agreements with the result that truly free contracts assure greater cohesion and cooperation. As Peter Drucker has noted,[7] workers can be attached strongly even to poor programs and procedures if they are their own.

The reason for demanding bilateral agreements in many areas is not economic but ethical. The mere ownership of property or the control of it does not bestow complete authority over the workers who handle the property, nor does the power to exact consent to working conditions constitute a legitimate right to extort them. Furthermore, as Drucker has pointed out, there are areas where management may not even be competent to make the decisions.[8] While it is not the function of an introductory book to explore all these questions in depth, students of business must realize that such questions must be considered before business can solve many of its ethical and economic problems.

[7] Peter F. Drucker, *The New Society* (New York, Harper & Row, 1949), p. 301.
[8] *Ibid.*, p. 280-316.

4

Wages and Working Conditions

INTRODUCTION

The ethics of hiring, firing, and promotions are largely a question of equal treatment of persons having equal job qualifications. The ethics of wages and working conditions are not so simple. They involve not only job qualifications, but the worker's human needs and the functioning of the economy as a whole. Because so many factors enter into the ethical judgment of the fairness of wages and the decency of working conditions, many thinkers despair of establishing any principles. Granted that there are few fixed guide lines, we still need some frame of reference lest management and labor settle disputes on the basis of power rather than in terms of at least a minimal justice.

WAGES VERSUS INCOME

Most discussions of the fair wage start with the assumption that wages are or ought to be the principal if not the only source of a worker's income. This leads to the conclusion that the fair wage ought to be sufficient to permit the worker and his family to live in decent comfort according to the increasing standards of society.

This comfort includes the possibility of making some provision for sickness and old age as well as for the education of children.

In an ideal world, the fair wage would certainly measure up to the minimum described above. In the real world, even in the very wealthy real world of the American economy, the ideal faces great obstacles. For the businessman, wages are a cost to be kept down or at best an incentive used to increase production. If he adds proper differentials to the ideal minimum, he will often have to price himself out of the market or replace workers with machines. Even if the ideal minimum *wage* is possible in some cases, it may not supply a decent minimum *income* for long. The worker may manage his money poorly and fail to make provision for sickness and old age. Inflation may rob wages of their purchasing power and raise the minimum level of money income necessary for decent comfort.

These facts lead to two conclusions. First, *income* rather than *wages* is the significant concept. Secondly, an adequate income cannot be supplied without broad social cooperation and some political control. As a result, the problem and the ideal are only partially the responsibility of business. Although this has not been completely accepted in theory, it has been recognized in practice. Social Security, Unemployment Compensation, compulsory accident insurance, medical assistance to the aged, public education, free lunch programs for children, and, in some nations, family allowances for children are all social means used to help workers arrive at a *minimum income* no matter how low their wages. There are numerous signs that we will be increasingly involved in this sort of government program.

FAIR WAGES[1]

In view of all this, the fairness of wages cannot, in practice, be established solely in terms of the needs of workers and their families. This does not mean, however, that wages are to be de-

[1] There is vast literature on this subject. Older treatments can be found in Frank Chapman Sharp and Philip G. Fox, *Business Ethics* (New York, Appleton-Century-Crofts, 1937) and Franz Mueller, "Some Thoughts on the Problem of Family Wages," in Richard Mulcahy, ed., *Readings in Economics* (Westminster, Md., Newman, 1959), p. 231-145; John F. Cronin, *Social Principles in Economic Life* (Milwaukee, Bruce, 1959), pp. 209 ff. My own thinking has been greatly in-

termined exclusively in terms of the market for labor or of the contribution of workers to the company. The market for labor can be manipulated in a variety of ways, and it is almost impossible to measure the actual contributions of workers. Demand, supply, and contribution do enter into the question, but they do not establish a complete norm of fairness.

In the opinion of the present writer, there is no *a priori* way of determining what constitutes a just wage or salary. Anyone familiar with the maze of wage and salary administration will agree. Wages must be related to the contribution to the firm, to the market for both labor and products, to the competitive position of the company, and to the power of the unions as well as to the needs of workers and their families. If any one of these factors is ignored, grave harm may result, no matter how good the intentions of management. All of these factors establish demands and limiting conditions. They create a framework of concrete and limited possibilities within which justice is to be found.

Since we have not worked out any satisfactory mathematical formula which will determine the proper weight to be given to all factors in all circumstances, it seems that a fair wage, as distinguished from a fair income, can be determined only by a fair work contract. A fair work contract will generally depend on the existence of *free and fair negotiations* which respect the positions of all parties involved. This is a big order, since in many cases consumers and society at large have a very big stake in wage negotiations. The concept, however, is sound, even though we have not evolved a social mechanism for taking care of the interests of third parties.

A contract is truly fair when both sides are free and conscious of the implications of their acts. Freedom does not imply that the contracting parties are overjoyed, but that their agreement is reasonable. The agreement is not reasonable, and there is no true freedom if one or both sides have used fraud, power, passion, or ignorance to bring about an agreement which would have been otherwise rejected. To be sure, the impairment of freedom must be substantial to vitiate a contract and make it truly unfair, but it can occur. Starv-

fluenced by the following very short articles: Edward Duff, "The Living Wage, A Note," *Social Order*, Vol. 5 (1955), pp. 294-298, and "The Living Wage, A Further Note," *Social Order*, Vol. 7 (1957), pp. 77-85; and Michael P. Fogarty, "Family Living Wages, A Comment," *Social Order*, Vol. 5 (1955), pp. 461-462.

ing workers will agree to almost anything to keep their children alive. A company which cannot afford a strike may have to submit to demands short of those which will cause immediate bankruptcy. In short, power can be substituted for reason and destroy even the minimal freedom needed for a fair contract. In our economy, where large companies and large unions are mingled with small companies, small unions, and no unions at all, the possibility of unfairness in a substantial degree is all too great.

Since we have no really adequate social means of assuring even approximate equality and freedom between all bargaining agents, fair agreements may often be accidents or exceptions rather than the rule. Indeed, because we are dealing with men, we need special efforts on the part of employers, workers and unions, and some social control which affects the areas untouched by organized labor or vitiated by power imbalances. As already noted, the shifting power positions of companies and unions may also make it necessary to provide institutions which allow consumers and other vitally interested parties to be represented.

While the ultimate solution to the problem of fair wages still lies in the future, in practice employers can at least check their wages against the following points:

1. The going *wage* in an industry and area when this is publicly accepted as "just."
2. The adequacy of the worker's *income* in terms of minimum standards such as those set by the Department of Labor.
3. The concrete possibility of helping the worker to a more adequate income.

The going wage in an industry and area which is publically accepted as "just" supplies a rough norm of fairness unless it has been set largely as a result of power, fraud, passion, or ignorance. If an employer is paying substantially below this going wage for a given job in an area, he ought to question the fairness of his wage contract. Similarly, if employers have agreed to keep wages low, and succeed because labor is poorly organized, the fairness of the contract is questionable.

While the going wage can provide a rough rule of thumb, it is not a final norm. The aim of society is still an income which will provide security and a decent living. If the going wage and other sources of income still leave large groups of employees below the minimum level, the businessman must do his share in helping society to provide all with a minimum decent income.

The businessman has two responsibilities in this area. First, he should cooperate with other groups in raising the social sources of income. Secondly, he should strive to make his business so efficient that he can raise the going rates to a point where they and other sources of income are adequate for decent living. This means that although the contractual wage may be fair in one sense, the businessman as a citizen and manager has obligations beyond the minimum of the contract. These are shared obligations and limited ones, but they do exist.

Actually the worst offenders against the obligations just mentioned are schools and hospitals which not only pay low wages, but make little effort to raise them. Some businesses offend by moving to areas where they exploit cheap labor and beat down those who want to bargain as equals. While owners, stockholders, and consumers may have claims on a business, the demands of workers cannot and should not be ignored. Consumers must pay the true cost of what they buy. Stockholders must realize that as a general rule wages are closer to the necessities of life than dividends.

Some will object that the approach to the wage situation is too idealistic and that the accepted treatment is too favorable to employers because the practical norms, as opposed to the ideal ones, tend to justify the *status quo*. Both criticisms are fair and to the point. In defense it can only be said that there appears to be no other realistic solution except one that develops from an attainable minimum and moves toward an obligatory ideal.

PROFIT SHARING

The increased number of firms engaged in profit sharing raises the question of whether or not employees have a right to share in profits. The answer depends on one's definition of profits. However, no matter how profits are defined, it is generally held that when the employee is receiving a fair wage, he is not entitled to any additional money as a matter of strict right. The reason is simply that he has freely agreed to limit his claims in justice to the agreed wage. He may, of course, seek to change the wage contract in order to obtain a share of profits, provided, of course, that he does not use power or fraud. The employer is morally free to grant a new contract or not, so long as he is paying a just wage.[2]

The theory stated above is certainly applicable to the vast majority of companies. However, there appears to be a new situation developing in which workers may have a claim to some share in the profits in addition to their contractual provisions. In the case of the company which no one owns in any real sense (although the stockholders may hold legal title of some sort), contribution rather than contract may be the only realistic title to income. In such companies the worker may, because of his contribution and cooperation within a sort of open contract, have a claim to share in the surplus to the extent that he has contributed to it. As yet, thinking has not advanced far enough to make this type of claim very precise. However, the student should anticipate its occurrence.

STABILITY OF WORK

Insecurity in employment has been one of the major factors leading to unionization. The reason is simply that man fears insecurity as much as he fears poverty. This is a reasonable fear since a man cannot order his own life or provide for the future if he is in doubt as to the security of his work and income. Although union negotiations and unemployment compensation have done much to mitigate the evils of insecurity, the problem will become more acute. Automation, the growth of seasonal industries, and plant relocations threaten security.

Although stable production would be in their own best interests, employers have resigned themselves to periodic layoffs and seasonal variations as a fact of economic life. However, the obligation to run a business efficiently and to avoid harmful impacts on others creates an obligation to work for the stabilization of production and employment. Realistically, such stability often depends on

[2] Benjamin L. Masse, S.J., "The Ethics of Profit Sharing," in William T. Greenwood, ed., *Issues in Business and Society* (Boston, Houghton Mifflin, 1964), pp. 57-62. Anyone interested in this area should consult the extensive literature supplied by the Center for Productivity Motivation School of Commerce, The University of Wisconsin, Madison, Wisconsin, as well as by the Profit Sharing Research Council.

factors beyond the direct control of the individual employer. Industry custom, technological advances, and the general state of the economy often dictate the level of production at a given time. These facts do not excuse the employer from his obligation, but transform it into a duty to work with others in producing an overall pattern of stability.

Concretely, employers must cooperate in planning on a broader social level. Planning may be a dirty word for many, but it is only asking businessmen to concede to society the rational approach of the employer within his firm. Some may object that planning involves a loss of freedom. This is a debatable question. The real concern is whether or not planning would be beneficial in the advancement of human well-being and freedom.

Later in this book we shall return to these questions, but even at the beginning it is important to realize that there are problems in business ethics which cannot be solved without broad social cooperation in industry and in the economy as a whole. Too often business ethics has been studied as if it had no social dimension and as if the businessman could bring about social justice on his own. Unless the total social and economic system is examined, we shall have only excuses and no solutions to even such a fundamental problem as that of wages.

WORKING CONDITIONS

The American experience with labor relations indicates that working conditions are as significant an area as wages and work stability. Despite this, it is all too easy to overlook the ethical problems by accepting—as right and just—situations which exist and always have existed. Legislation and conscience have solved many problems. We should not forget, however, that in the past, mine donkeys were better cared for than miners. Even today there are cases where migrant workers are housed like animals with little or no consideration given to the health and education of their children.

A worker should not be treated as a thing. Neither should he or his family be exposed to physical, psychological, or moral harm without a proportionate reason. To disregard safety in these areas is to disregard the good of a human being and even the simplest ethical principles. There are cases where nothing can be done to eliminate risks or where the cost of eliminating them may be prohibitive, but the general principle stands: safety is ethically important.

Cases involving risk of physical harm are obvious; there is no need to cite them. Psychological and moral dangers are liable to be overlooked. A few illustrations will alert managers to the type of situations they must try to avoid. Interestingly enough, these same situations generally contain elements which are detrimental to the efficient functioning of the business itself.

Poor cash and inventory control systems can tempt workers to steal. Therefore, both good ethics and good business require that reasonable measures be taken for the protection of the worker and the firm. Similarly, new workers should be warned of the ethical pitfalls connected with their jobs and be assured of the firm's stand on principles. This might seem naive, but many a new employee is corrupted by being involved in bribery or theft before he knows what is happening. Also, the office clique may fill the vacuum left by management and establish its own policies which may harm both company and worker.

Managers and supervisors might also keep their eyes open for more serious schemes which exploit the gullible in their employ. There are individuals who use a place of business to sell tickets for fraudulent lotteries. There are occasional supervisors who use their staff as part of an informal harem. There are scoundrels who coerce the timid into cooperating in all sorts of unethical practices under the threat of false denunciation and subsequent dismissal. While there are no statistics on the frequency of such occurrences, my own consulting work indicates that these situations are not rarities.

The boss is not an almighty father who can or should control the private morals of his employees, but he certainly cannot be indifferent to what goes on in his firm. If he recalls the confusion and loneliness of his own first weeks at work, he may realize that young workers need advice, help, and protection. He should be aware that the type of situation we have been describing is not conducive to high levels of morale and efficiency. If he fails to act, he gives tacit approval to favoritism, office politics, featherbedding, and conspiracy in theft.

Managers on all levels should remember that their power to

command, reward, and punish, is not self-justifying. It carries with it a responsibility to use power for the good of the company, with due respect for the rights and consciences of others. Forcing, ordering, or encouraging employees to act unethically or to cooperate in unethical activities, is doubly wrong, for the manager who does this should remember that he has not only harmed another human being but has taught him that the manager himself is not worthy of trust.

Working conditions can affect both the home life and family finances. While an employer is not directly responsible for such effects in the vast majority of cases, he should consider them and the offsetting goods. The man who is constantly on the road will have grave difficulties in fulfilling his duties as father and husband. Although travel is a part of the employee's job, the ethical employer will ask if all the travel is necessary in view of the effects on the wife and children.

Job transfers can involve considerable expense and even increased living costs. While the employer can often force the worker to pay these, conscientious firms will make appropriate allowances for both transportation and cost of living adjustments. This is a question of fairness and of good internal relations.

The list of situations involving detrimental impacts on workers and their families might be almost endless. A complete catalogue, however, can say no more than that the impacts should be considered, since a man is not a thing but a human being with his own rights and dignity.

WORK SATISFACTION[3]

Recent studies have shown that although good wages may keep people from complaining, they do not motivate workers as successfully as work satisfaction. For this reason, employers have an economic interest in work satisfaction. There are, however, deeper human considerations involved. Work occupies a large part of a man's day. Unless his job is humanly satisfying, not only his productivity but his whole life is diminished. Man needs to find significance in what he does. Unconsciously, at least, he needs to feel that he has

3 See Thomas M. Garrett, S.J., *Ethics in Business* (New York, Sheed, 1963), pp. 46-62, and the note on page 62 in particular.

created something, served others, and left his mark upon the world. Work should provide the opportunity for this sense of fulfillment.

Since both employers and employees have an important stake in work satisfaction, there is certainly an obligation to consider this aspect of business. Lack of imagination and initiative can contribute to moral failures as well as business losses. While it is difficult to be more specific, it would certainly appear that the businessman has a real obligation to study and utilize the vast literature concerned with motivation.

Unless this very human side of business is appreciated and studied, the executive may discover that highly efficient technological innovations have been frustrated by unhappy human beings whose sense of justice has been offended. It will also be clear to the knowledgeable reader that both the obligation to respect workers and the obligation to run an efficient firm can be fulfilled only by the truly competent manager who has both technical skill and human sensitivity. The study of managerial and industrial psychology is ethically imperative, but human sensitivity will not result from mere textbook knowledge. The first-class manager must also know himself, his own fears, limitations, and values if he is to respect others and compensate for his own deficiencies. Only in this way can he be sure that his perception of the needs and rights of others has not been distorted by selfishness and by a narrow view of the function of management.

5

Private Lives
and Company Lives

INTRODUCTION

In the days of the company town, everyone knew where he stood even if he did not like it. The company controlled the plant, the stores, the credit, the real estate, and the political machine. If someone was dissatisfied, he could move out of town. This situation has changed for the better in America, but similar problems still exist.

1. Does a firm have a right to demand that workers contribute to the Community Chest?
2. Does a firm have a right to force employees into civic activities?
3. Can a firm ethically limit the political activity of employees?
4. Is it ethical to impose personality and lie detector tests and to "bug" the rest room?

All of these questions center on a single problem which may be phrased in various ways. Where does an employee's company life end and his private life begin? To what extent may a company legitimately limit the employee's freedom in areas that have traditionally been considered private? Since many companies have the power to interfere a great deal, we are not asking whether or not they can do these things, but whether or not it is ethical and just to do them.

RISE OF THE PROBLEM

The old-style paternalist had no doubts about his rights since he assumed that everything was his business and that his workers were his children. While this view was accepted by workers, there was no protest and therefore, little consideration of the problem. Similarly, the man who viewed his workers as so many hands to produce physical labor had few worries about his rights. He simply fired a man when he did not produce and replaced him with another.

The problem is acute when the manager realizes that productivity is controlled by more than muscle and that the company reputation is an important source of profits. The new manager generally realizes that he is not the father of a family, but research has shown him that many aspects of a worker's life and personality do influence the good of the company. As a result, the manager has become more and more interested in areas that were once considered private. In addition, the development of sophisticated techniques has made it possible for the company to penetrate areas that were once more or less protected from all intrusion. The lie detector, the personality test, the electronic snooping device, efficient credit checks and private investigating services, have all created the possibility of probing at the very time when managers may feel that they have a legitimate interest in knowing everything that may influence production and profit.

Granted that a company does not own a man, but has a right only to specified services, we must still ask: Where is the line between legitimate and illegitimate interferences with what was once considered the private life of the employee? This really involves two questions. First, what areas may be legitimately investigated? Secondly, what means may be legitimately used?

THE VALUE OF PRIVACY

The questions posed above are difficult to answer not only because they involve complicated situations, but because many people see little or no value in privacy. We have become so accustomed to certain invasions of privacy that they are accepted as a matter of course. Yet, privacy is an important value which can be manifested in three areas: the psychic, the physical, and the social.

The most basic and sacred privacy is psychic. It is the privacy of the inner sphere, of man's thoughts, ideals, ambitions, and feelings. It is the area of personality which is especially human and especially personal. Indeed, so intimate is the union between this sphere and the person that it is often impossible to distinguish them. While there are levels of privacy and therefore room for distinctions, the essential point should be clear: the psychic sphere belongs to man in a special way and demands a special respect.

An individual manifests his inner life in many ways. Gestures, handwriting, facial expressions, and language reveal edges of the psychic sphere. In addition, individuals may want to reveal other areas to those who can help them or to those whom they love. In general, however, most of us keep large areas concealed not only from the general public, but even from those who are close to us. There are good reasons for such secrecy. In the first place, it protects us from exploitation at the hands of those who might want to use us for their own purposes. In the second place, indiscriminate revelation of the inner sphere can disturb both the individual and those who receive his confidences. For these reasons, an individual has the right and often the obligation to protect his psychic privacy. Others have a corresponding obligation to respect this inner sphere.

By the very nature of the case, the rights to psychic privacy are not absolute. A man may be obliged to reveal his inner life to a psychologist if this is necessary for his own mental health. For good and sufficient reason, a man may choose to reveal himself to another. An employer may even have the right to ask for the revelation of some inner life if this is necessary for the protection of the individual, his fellow workers, or the company. Such need, however, ought to be established rather than assumed.

Physical privacy is a necessary means to the protection of psychic privacy. Unless there are times and places where a man can share his inner sphere with those he loves or those who will help him, he will be deprived of many necessary goods. Husband and wife, doctor and patient, lawyer and client, employer and employee —all need the protection of physical privacy if they are to do their jobs.

Some courts have decided that physical privacy is violated only by direct physical trespass. According to these, spying through binoculars or by means of microphones outside the owner's property is not a violation of the owner's privacy. This is a narrow and dangerous view, for modern techniques can cause the harm without direct physical trespass. A man's right to privacy is not bounded by his property lines. Actually, the right to privacy has nothing to do with property in the ordinary sense. It is rather a right concerned with the protection of feelings and personal relations and with the physical conditions necessary to protect these.[1]

The right to such privacy is not absolute, but law has recognized its existence. Even the police cannot search a man's home except in carefully delineated circumstances. We have laws against the Peeping Tom. Our society has always condemned the nosy person because of the harm which ensues from idle snooping and gossiping. At the same time, we recognize that spying is legitimate in time of war, since the right of one group to privacy is limited by the right of the other group to protect itself against unjust attack.

Not merely psychic and physical privacy, but social role privacy is necessary for the individual and society. Each of us must play a number of roles if society is to function efficiently. Thus, an individual must be a father, a husband, and a citizen, as well as an administrator if he is to fulfill all of his duties. Often he cannot do this unless the roles are separated and insulated one from the other. For example, as a citizen a man may be obliged to protest something which the business community favors. If he cannot separate his roles, the political community may lose a valuable leader. So too, the manager of a firm does not want the fear of reprisals against his family to interfere with his sound business judgment. While role distinctions cannot be maintained completely, the breakdown of barriers can cause very great harm. As a result, secrecy and privacy are needed as supports of role distinction.

At very least, privacy is necessary in order to protect the individual from self-incrimination and from the destruction of his reputation. As a result, even when there are legitimate reasons for invad-

---

[1] The law in this area is changing. The reader should consult Samuel H. Hofstadter and George Horowitz, *The Right of Privacy* (New York, Central Book, 1964) or the more popular book of William Zelermyer, *Invasion of Privacy* (Syracuse, Syracuse University Press, 1959).

ing privacy, there is always an obligation to protect the individual as much as possible.

With these points in mind, we can return to our original questions. What areas of the employee's private world may be ethically investigated by the company? What means may be ethically used to conduct the investigation?

AREAS OF LEGITIMATE INTEREST

A firm is legitimately interested in whatever influences *work performance in any significant way*. After all, the company does pay for the employee's work even though it cannot buy or lease the worker himself.

Heavy drinking, heavy gambling by a controller and loose talk by key employees are pertinent to job performance, but a man's fidelity in marriage or membership in a nudist camp are not. There are in-between cases too, but the company should look to the significance of the relationship lest it involve itself in the gathering of all sorts of expensive data which has little bearing on the job. Very often even information about emotional stability or aspirations may have little predictive value, since it is difficult to say how a man will react in a specific situation and to specific co-workers. Tests developed for clinical use may help in weeding out obvious misfits, but they may give little information about positive job performance. There is need for considerable reserve lest an unfounded enthusiasm for tests cause companies to pry deeper than is their right.[2] Furthermore, an interest in details beyond the truly significant can arouse hostility in workers who will rightly feel that the company is trying to run their entire life. The fact that the interest is legitimate, however, does not mean that all means of gathering data are justified.

The more difficult problems arise in regard to dealing with private acts and information which affect the *company image*. The problem is particularly great since, as a man mounts the ladder of the company hierarchy, the influence of his activities on the company image are often significant for work performance. If a mill worker belongs to the Communist Party, the job performance is not

---

[2] Thomas M. Garrett, S.J., *Ethics in Business* (New York, Sheed, 1963), pp. 97-109, treats the ethics of personality testing.

affected, and the effect on the company image is probably negligible. If a vice-president belongs to the American Nazi Party, the situation is different, since people may not want to deal with him or with a company that has such a man in a key position. This could be true even if the executive does not identify his public acts with the company.

Even though a company may at times have a legitimate interest in private activities which affect the *image* and the workings of the company, this does not mean that it can ethically interfere with these activities. Company control of its employees' political activity may not be healthy for the nation and the community. It can slow down change and free debate, and favor the *status quo*. Furthermore, unless there is a clear policy and provision for due process, decisions may be arbitrary. To put it another way, the fact of citizenship in the firm should not deprive a man of his rights to fair treatment and his right to participate in the general political life of the nation. Labor law protects workers in this area, but management people do not have the same benefits. Companies, then, should make sure that their interference is really necessary and not the result of emotionalism or short-sighted selfishness.

Often privacy is disregarded not in the condemnation of outside activities, but in the "encouragement" of civic participation which will improve executive skills and the company image and power. The aspiring young executive may be told—if not actually commanded—to run for the school board, head up the Community Chest Drive, or become active in some worthwhile civic activity. Generally speaking, the community may benefit from this, but does the company have the right to bring real pressure to bear? Similarly, does a company have a right to force contributions to charity or political parties in the interest of the company reputation? Where does legitimate persuasion end and polite blackmail begin? Although each case will be highly individual, I would suggest that the following are sound guide lines.

In general, the assumption ought to be that the individual's right is primary and that there should not be unreasonable interference. The reasonableness of the interference, however, cannot be determined unilaterally, since self-interest blinds. This is to say that solid ethical norms in this area can only be established by a form of collective bargaining.

For many businesses, there is an additional problem. Modern business involves a great deal of traveling. The need for this is well understood by employees and accepted as a part of their working conditions. The word *need* must be stressed, for time spent away from home creates problems which can be justified only if the traveling is necessary. If the effects on wife and children are completely disregarded, a company may be acting as if it owned not only the employee, but his family as well. Once again precise norms may be impossible, but there is certainly an obligation to consider the effects of travel on the private lives of employees.

GARNISHMENTS

Although many employers are not concerned about the problems we have mentioned above, there is considerable worry about the problem of garnishments. A garnishment involves the legal attachment of wages for payment of debts. It forces the company to act as a collection agency for some debtor who has received a legal judgment against an employee. Most of the time, the existence of a garnishment will also indicate that the employee is a bad credit risk.

Some companies have a policy of firing an employee after the second garnishment. At first glance, this might seem like an unwarranted interference with private life. However, this is not the case when there is an explicit company policy. The company rightfully objects to its accounting costs being increased by the carelessness of employees. For this reason, the garnishment, though it may not pertain to job performance, certainly affects the good of the company and not merely its image.

THE MEANS OF INVESTIGATION

Although a company may have a legitimate interest in many of its employees' activities, not all means of investigation are ethical. Privacy, as noted previously, has its claims, even though they are not absolute in either ethics or war. In taking a job, the employee certainly surrenders part of his privacy. He agrees to *ordinary* supervision of his work and to *ordinary* investigation of his suitability for the position. The ethical problem is concerned with the often hazy line between the ordinary and reasonable and the extraordinary and unreasonable interference with privacy. In the concrete, what means are reasonable in what circumstances? Can a company use wire taps, hidden television, polygraph tests, and personality testing, or are these ruled out because they are not common and ordinary?

Here as in the previous pages, the benefit of the doubt belongs to the employee; the right to use less common methods of surveillance and investigation must be justified by a proportionate reason. We might ask, for example, if some less questionable action would suffice to protect the firm and the rights of honest workers. The manager might also ask himself if honest employees would freely cooperate if they knew what was at stake. The first question considers the necessity of the measure for the social good of the firm and the protection of a worker's more basic rights. The second question is concerned with whether or not the surveillance may be considered a reasonable part of the work contract itself.

If wiring a *work area* is necessary to prevent thefts which cannot be controlled by ordinary means, I would tend to think that the company had a proportionate reason. Wiring might be necessary when employees were handling small valuable items such as drugs or diamonds. Even in these cases, the existence of the wiring should be known to the workers so that they may protect their legitimate secrets. The use of spies or secret wiring in the work area or of *any devices in such non-work areas* as lounges and rest rooms would require far more serious reasons. These should be of the type required for the authorization of a search warrant; there should be the founded suspicion that the procedure will unearth evidence of a serious crime which has already occurred. The neurotic suspicion that something might be discovered or the desire to pick up a useful tid-bit do not constitute reasonable grounds for invading privacy.

Even when there are reasonable grounds for the use of the methods mentioned above, there remains an obligation to protect the workers from harmful side effects. There will be information about private lives and feelings collected in the big net, and these facts must be destroyed, forgotten, or disregarded, since the company has no right to collect and use such information. This may require considerable restraint if the boss discovers that his "admiring" secretary really thinks he is a fraud. Indeed, it is because the surveillance may turn up just this sort of information that grave reasons are needed to justify the risk.

The obligation to protect workers exists in other areas. It can be ethical to use lie detector tests in screening applicants for responsibilities such as handling controlled drugs and large sums of currency, but there is an obligation to hire a skilled polygraph operator and to interpret results with great caution. In addition, even valid results must either be destroyed or guarded so that their use is confined to those who really need the information for making decisions. We shall have more to say on this in Chapter Seven when we treat the obligation of secrecy.

The problem of personality testing has been treated at some length in *Ethics in Business*.[3] Here we wish only to recall some major conclusions with regard to interference with psychic privacy. As in the cases above, the invasion needs justification, since the right of the individual is primary. More extensive invasions require the free consent of the employee. All information must be interpreted only by competent people and used with reserve even when its use is necessary. Finally, results and data should be destroyed when the employee leaves the company and guarded carefully in the meantime.

TOWARD A SOLUTION

The right of the individual to privacy is primary and gives way only to the proven reasonableness of interference by either a company or society in general. In many cases privacy is necessary for the growth of the individual and the functioning of the group. Privacy permits us to enter into intimate relationships which would never occur in the public eye. It permits us to distinguish our roles and to keep separate those aspects of our lives which ought to be kept separate. The goods involved cannot be dismissed lightly. As a result, a company should ask itself if an interference is *necessary* since it is obvious that it can often be useful.

The use of force to interfere with privacy is a sure indication that injustice is involved except in those cases where an explicit and

[3] *Ibid.*

free contract has granted such authority to the employer. The use of blackmail, even in a good cause, is unethical. While it is difficult to distinguish between reasonable persuasion and blackmail, the extreme cases are clear enough. The in-between cases can sometimes be settled by asking the question, "Would I resent this being done to me?" The best method, of course, is to seek the advice of an honest and uninvolved outsider.

Actually, the best way to handle the gray area of privacy is by means of collective bargaining which results in an explicit contract. In many cases this bargaining is ethically necessary, since neither side has the information required to make a founded judgment of what is reasonable. Only an agreement based on careful discussion can result in even an approximately just and workable norm. Existing practice in either a company or an industry is not necessarily a good norm, since it may have resulted from unilateral decisions forced on a group which had no means of redress.

To insure justice, the norms developed by collective bargaining must also be subject to some form of due process lest arbitrary and unilateral interpretations and enforcement undo the bilateral agreement. Some people may look at this as an infringement of management rights. They forget, however, that management does not have rights over the workers by virtue of property ownership, but only through contract, or in some cases, popular consent. The manager is not the family's father, endowed by nature with authority over every aspect of his employees' lives.

In the last analysis, contracts and collective bargaining may not be sufficient to guarantee due process and fair treatment. In the *Government of Corporations*, Richard Eells has noted the need for a bill of rights which will protect employees against the private government of the firm just as the Constitution protects citizens against the civil rulers.[4] It may be, then, that we will not even approximate true justice in business until we have established some form of corporation constitutionalism which provides both the rules of the game and some form of outside review.

[4] Richard Eells, *The Government of Corporations* (New York, Free Press, 1962), p. 268.

III

*Relationship of
the Employee to the Firm*

6

Fiduciary Relationships and Conflicts of Interest

INTRODUCTION

The contract of employment creates obligations for the employee as well as the employer. Basically, the employee is bound to give an honest day's work for an honest day's wages. While this is true, it is neither a perfectly clear nor an all-inclusive statement of the employee's obligations to the firm. The present chapter and the two which follow attempt to spell out some of the duties which can easily be overlooked. In particular, these chapters will look at those duties which are implicit rather than clearly stated.

By the work contract the employee agrees to give a more or less specified amount of time, energy, and intelligence to the firm in return for income. While he does not subordinate himself as an individual, he does contract away some of his minor rights and agrees that these will be used for the benefit of the company which employs him. Providing the employer lives up to his side of the agreement, the employee, whether he be the president or the office boy, may not use the firm to gain personal advantages not provided for in the contract.

CONFLICTS OF INTEREST

The interest of the firm is not always identical with the interest of the employee. This should surprise no one, for interests seldom coincide completely in any sphere of life. In general, the employee will think it to his interest to get the greatest possible reward for his work. The employer, on the other hand, sees his interest as identified in part with getting the greatest possible productivity out of his men and machines. Because of this situation, the work contract is necessary to define the actual rights and interests of both parties. Each party gives up something in order to gain something. In this way some conflicts can be avoided or at least minimized.

Conflicts of interest may be either actual or potential. As a result, certain actions which are not immediately harmful to the firm may be unethical because they contain the potentiality of a real conflict of interest or the possibility of destroying the good order of an entire industry. An actual conflict of interest exists when an employee violates his contract of employment by using his position for selfish purposes which are at odds with the best interest of the firm. A purchasing agent who pays a higher price than necessary to a supplier from whom he has accepted a bribe is involved in an actual conflict of interest. On the other hand, a strong-minded man who accepts large gifts may never actually harm the company, but he is still involved in a potential conflict of interest since most men in this sort of situation find it difficult to maintain their independence of judgment in acting for the true good of the company.

In many conflict of interest cases, not only the rights of the company, but those of third parties are involved. It is necessary, then, to consider the impact of certain practices on parties outside the firm. For this reason the questions of extortion and payola are considered in the present chapter.

In studying conflicts of interest and related problems such as extortion, particular attention must be paid to the following:
1. The position of the individuals involved.
2. The intentions of all parties.
3. The impacts, potential and actual, on the parties, the company, and outside interests.
4. Company policy, whether written or oral.

BRIBERY, EXTORTION, AND GIFTS

The range of problems in this area of business ethics can be illustrated by a series of short cases, which contain nearly all of the relevant elements.

1. An art director for an advertising agency places his orders for supplies with a friend who "kicks back" a fixed percentage at the end of each month. The supplier's prices are fairly competitive, but the advertising agency does end up paying slightly more than necessary for its supplies.

The art director is accepting a *bribe* in taking a consideration for the performance of an act which is forbidden by his work contract. Even if his act did not cost the company money, he would be wrong since he is *cooperating* with another who intends to gain an unfair advantage, that is, preferential treatment which is not based on the merit of his product and prices. Since the company actually loses money because of this illegal contract, we are dealing with a form of *stealing*. Finally, such arrangements upset the orderly course of the industry and tempt others to engage in similar activities. The activity is also to be condemned because of its *broader effects*.

It should be noted that the method of payment does not change the intention or the effects of the bribery. Whether the consideration is in the form of cash, services, or privileges, we are dealing with bribery and a violation of the fiduciary relationship. Similarly, whether the consideration is given before or after the act, as a gift or as a loan which will never be repaid, the basic unethical quality remains so long as the intention is the same.

2. A purchasing agent will not even consider a salesman's offer unless he has received a substantial gift before hand. Often he buys from the salesman who offers the best price, delivery, and quality, but occasionally he tosses some business to less competitive companies in order to keep their salesmen as contributors to his vacation fund.

This case involves not only bribery, but *extortion*. Extortion exists when a man demands payment of any sort for the execution (or non-execution) of acts which he is obliged to perform or to omit under the terms of his work contract. Secondly, it is extortion to demand payment for the execution (or non-execution) of acts which a man has no right to perform or to omit by virtue of his position. In its severest form, extortion may involve the use of physical force. Extortion in its mildest form may only involve implied threats unrelated to true business considerations.

Extortion includes all the evils of bribery plus the violation of the salesman's right to fair and equal treatment based upon the merits of his product. It violates the relationship between employer and employee and that between buyer and seller as well. If the salesman had the best product and service, the purchasing agent was obliged to purchase from him without demanding personal profit. If the salesman did not offer the best deal to the company, the agent had no right to give him the order even after receiving the money he had extorted.

Even though the extortioner may not harm his company in each and every transaction, the overall effect is one of serious violation of the fiduciary relationship. Indeed, if extortion becomes widespread, it will almost certainly force prices upward as bribes become fixed parts of the selling costs. Not merely the individual acts, but the ramifications must be considered if the total evil effect is to be seen in all of its dimensions.

3. A department store manager accepts fairly substantial gifts, such as cases of liquor, from salesmen. He feels that these gifts do not prejudice his judgment. The company has a written policy against such gifts, but the manager justifies his actions on the ground that everyone does it.

Our third case does not necessarily involve either bribery or extortion. The manager does not intend to give favored treatment to those who fill his liquor cabinet, nor does he demand these gifts. It may even be that the salesmen do not intend to get favored treatment, but only want to make sure that they get equal treatment. So long as the situation remains exactly as described, there is no *actual* conflict of interest as we have defined it earlier. None of this, however, should blind one to the real evils in the situation. Not only is there a *potential* conflict of interest, but there is a direct violation of company policy and of the work contract. The fact that others engage in the same practice increases rather than decreases his obligation to avoid accepting substantial gifts. His act sanctions the acts of others who, unknown to him, may be involved in bribery, extortion, and real conflicts of interest. To put it another way, the store manager has an obligation to protect the best interests of the company by his good example as well as by his good intentions.

The salesmen may or many not intend their gifts as bribes. The manager has no reason for risking cooperation with what may be bribery. By his actions he is cooperating in the perpetuation of a system which contributes nothing to good business and may be the breeding ground of seriously unethical practices.

Our case was fairly simple since the gifts were substantial, and there was an explicit company policy forbidding all gifts. When there is no clear policy we are faced with questions like the following: At what point does a gift become so large or substantial that accepting it creates a potential conflict of interest? Under what circumstances, if any, does an employee have a proportionate reason for running the risks involved in accepting gifts? While there are no easy answers to these questions, the following considerations may be useful.[1]

This basic question should be asked: Will this gift, entertainment, or service cause any reasonable person to suspect my independence of judgment? It should be clear that infrequent gifts of only a nominal cost, ten dollars or less, and small advertisement gifts will be acceptable unless forbidden by policy or law. On the other hand, practically any cash gift is liable to raise eyebrows and create a suspicion of bias.

The law, of course, should be consulted since there are statutory provisions making all gift giving and receiving illegal in government contracting and in some states.[2] Similarly, the ethical codes of some lesgislatures have provisions on this subject.

Entertainment may be judged by similar norms. Industry custom may supply some guide lines, but one should be constantly aware of avoiding obligations which would hamper that independence of judgment necessary for fulfilling the responsibilities of the job. Some companies seek to minimize the problem by requiring employees to pick up the tab and turn it in for reimbursement. Others believe that reciprocity in entertainment will mitigate potential conflicts of interest. There is something to be said for both of

[1] "Ensuring Ethical Conduct in Business," *The Conference Board Record,* Vol. 1 (December, 1964), pp. 23-27, gives several examples of existing policies in the area of gift giving and entertainment.

[2] *Ibid.,* p. 24, cites the law governing gifts by and to government contractors.

these solutions, but reciprocity may merely authorize the mutual luncheon club in which members alternate in picking up the tab whether or not any *bona fide* business transaction has been involved.

In all cases of doubt, it is possible to get a ruling from the appropriate supervisor. If this includes full and honest disclosure of the problem, the employee has demonstrated his good faith by exposing his actions to surveillance. Many companies demand such disclosures as a standard procedure and though it is not a panacea, it prevents the development of many dangerous situations. If nothing else, consultation and disclosure relieve the employee of nagging doubts and protect him against the deceptions of those who might want to involve him in a potential conflict of interest.

4. A salesman who would never think of offering a bribe on his own finds himself dealing with a customer who will not give serious consideration to an offer unless his palm has been greased. He makes a contribution justifying himself on the grounds that he must earn a living and is not really hurting the business.

Our fourth sample case involves cooperation with the unethical conduct of a customer who has resorted to extortion. While such cases may be solved on the principles given in Chapter Two, certain warnings are in order. The person cooperating may not *will* the harm as a means to his own ends. In judging whether or not he has a sufficient reason to *permit* the harm, the potential injury to the industry as well as to a particular company must be considered. Further, just making a sale is not a proportionate reason, for the salesman's livelihood does not depend on getting this particular business. Finally, a *narrow* self-interest should always be suspected and countered lest easy rationalizations be used to excuse everything that suits one's fancy.

Cases of unethical cooperation often baffle younger businessmen, since they may sense that something is wrong, but they lack the experience to identify the evil. They might remember that contact with evil tends to corrupt and caution is seldom out of order. At the same time, even the cautious man must realize that there are circumstances in which serious harm or the threat of it may justify his cooperating indirectly in a morally unsound transaction. The case we have just given cannot be solved without more information. However, the existence of a proportionate reason should be *proved rather than assumed*.

PAYOLA

The term payola has been used so loosely that it covers not only bribery, extortion, and violations of fiduciary relationships, but some quite legitimate forms of exchange. As a result, one must look behind the label for the reality. The promotion man who supplies a new automobile for use in a moving picture benefits both his client and the movie producer. He has not injured the interests of any third party. On the other hand, a disk jockey who accepts a personal "gift" for plugging a song violates the interests of several groups. He probably deceives his listeners by concealing his true personal judgment, and he denies equal and fair treatment to competing song writers and record companies. In some cases, he uses previously purchased advertising time to the advantage of someone who has not paid the station for its services. Finally, the disk jockey pockets money which belongs to his employer, if it belongs to anyone.

FINANCIAL AND OTHER INTERESTS

Sound ethics and many company policies seek to minimize potential conflicts of interest in the relations between supplier and producer as well as between agent and client. Typical company policies, for example, contain provisions like the following promulgated by the International Harvester Company.[3]

Thus, it is considered to be in conflict with the Company's interest:
b . . . for an employee or member of his immediate family to benefit personally from any purchase of goods or services of whatever nature by the Company or its affiliates, or to derive personal gain from actions taken or associations made in his capacity as an employee of the Company;
c . . . for an employee or member of his immediate family to have any interest, direct or indirect, in any organization which has business dealings with the Company or any affiliate, except when such interest comprises securities in widely held corporations and traded regularly in recognized

[3] *Business Ethics* (A collection of documents compiled by the Research and Information Service of the American Management Association, 1963), p. 12.

security markets, and such interest is not in excess of 1% of the outstanding stock or other securities of such corporation, or except when such interest has been fully disclosed to the President of the Company for a determination as to the substantiality of such interest and the propriety of retaining it;

d . . . for an employee to serve as an officer, director, employee or consultant of another company or organization which is a competitor of the Company or which is doing or seeking to do business with the Company or any affiliate, except that with the knowledge and consent of the President of the Company such employee may serve as a director of a corporation which is doing business with the Company, where no competitive situation is present;

The theory behind such policies should be obvious. Management and employees should avoid actual violations of their fiduciary relationships and situations which might weaken their independence of judgment and action. It should be noted that policies generally provide for exceptions which can be granted by the president and/or directors. There are reasons for this. No company wants to restrict its employees unnecessarily, and there are cases where the company itself can benefit by its employees' having interests in other companies.

The most subtle conflicts, both actual and potential, arise not because of a direct financial interest, but because of friendship or family loyalty. The problem is all the more difficult since both of these factors can often play a legitimate part in business. At the same time, there is danger that one hand may wash the other while the company's face gets dirty. It is not only a question of nepotism in hiring and leaking inside information, but in giving out orders and making promotions on the basis of sentiment rather than of merit. Except in a family business, fairness to the company, employees, competing suppliers, and customers, makes friendship and family suspect.

MOONLIGHTING

Paragraph (d) in the International Harvester policy points out several areas where moonlighting is or can be hostile to company interests. Although the greatest problems arise when the second job is with a company that competes or deals with the primary employer, nearly all outside employment may involve some potential conflicts. If nothing else, a second job drains away energy, impairs efficiency, and divides interests. This does not mean that moonlighting is necessarily unethical. In many cases the employee has no choice. He must meet his obligations to his family, and therefore, barring an actual conflict of interest, he may have adequate reason for giving less than his all to the primary employer. Studies of moonlighting among policemen indicate that such activities can actually reduce the efficiency of the worker in his main job to almost nothing.[4] Employers might give some thought to the fact that they get what they pay for and that they may be robbing themselves by underpaying their employees.

PREVENTING CONFLICTS OF INTEREST

Because there are so many gray areas, explicit company policy is useful if not absolutely necessary. Such policies will hardly deter the dishonest, but they give the decent individual concrete norms which he can use in forming his values and in defending himself against pressures. If nothing else, the employee can give clear reasons for rejecting suspicious proposals.

Many companies try to lessen potential conflicts of interest by demanding from employees full disclosure of ownership in outside companies or of other relationships which might influence independence of judgment. Such disclosures can be of considerable help, but it probably needs to be reinforced by periodic independent checks. In addition, the policy should be explicit so as to include all important sources of potential conflicts. Unfortunately, this may be impossible, for it is hard to legislate friendship and all family ties out of existence. At very least, one can try to explicate as clearly as possible the areas of danger which might require disclosure.

Often the temptation to become involved with conflicting interests is strongest for middle executives such as assistant purchasing agents or assistant department heads whose income may not be really

4 Ralph Lee Smith, *The Tarnished Badge* (New York, Crowell, 1965), pp. 61-62.

commensurate with their responsibility and power. Since adequate pay can reduce this danger, companies should give serious consideration to this idea. Furthermore, a system of checks and balances in critical areas would seem to be in order. If even petty cash slips are a part of the company's standing control procedure, sensitive areas should be subject to some valid system of checks and balances.

As several studies have shown, the best protection is the example presented by the conduct of top management and the atmosphere it creates. When leaders are scrupulous, employees know what is considered right. When example is supported by explicit policy, the followers have a clear idea of how to translate the example of leaders into action. When policy is enforced and enforcement reinforced, the employees know that honesty is the best policy in this company.

EXECUTIVE PIRACY

We place the problem of executive piracy in the present chapter, since most of the cases which are unethical involve inducing a breach of contract or a violation of the fiduciary relationship. When the piracy has as its purpose the theft of secrets or the crippling of a competitor's business, there is no doubt about the unethical quality of the act. The real problems arise in those cases where the motive is not so clearly unethical.

When piracy involves tempting a man to break a formal and explicit contract, it is generally unethical. However, if the recruiter and recruitee are only asking for a reconsideration and possibly a release from a contract, this can be ethical since an employee does not lose the right to renegotiate and ask for release. Sometimes, we meet cases where the present employer has fulfilled all the technical parts of a work contract, but violated its spirit. Ethically, I believe the employee in such circumstances is free to enter into a contract with a new employer. The legal aspects, however, need study by a lawyer. If we exclude the intention of hurting a competitor, I believe recruiters are ethically free to approach those ethically free to enter into a new contract.

Special problems arise when there is no formal agreement or contract but only a sort of vague understanding which neither party regards as absolutely obligatory. To what extent is such an understanding binding in ethics if not in law? The employee, as we have noted in a previous chapter, has a reasonable expectation that he will not be fired except for just cause. So too, the employer has reasonable expectations that his personnel will not leave without good reason. This expectation can be particularly strong when the employer has taken on the burden of training and has kept on an employee through rough times. While such factors may not create a legal obligation in the absence of a formal contract, they certainly enter into the calculation of proportionality.

The factors mentioned above are often outweighed by both individual and social reasons. It is important that human resources be allocated properly and not frozen in a position where their true economic and creative potential cannot be fully realized. Furthermore, unless the employee has some freedom to better himself, the employment contract might be a modern form of peonage. Legally, people can enter into contracts which stipulate that they are not to compete for a period of time or in a given area. Thus the employment contract may contain a provision that an employee may not work for a rival during a period of two years after the termination of his job. If the contract was truly free and legal, there is an obligation to observe it. We should, however, recognize the possibility that this may not be in the true public interest.

Non-recruiting pacts, like blacklists, are socially harmful, possibly illegal, and potentially unjust to employees.[5] Indeed, unless companies are challenged to make the best use of their human resources, they too may suffer from tired managerial blood. Furthermore, unless there are periodic occasions where the market sets the price of management talent, a company can be underpaying a man. Actually, many problems in this area may be mitigated if a company has a policy of using formal contracts which are temporarily binding; they allow the company to recover its recruiting and training costs, and give it the option of matching *bona fide* offers from other companies. While such contractual provisions are not a final solution, they do help to regularize the expectations of both employee and employer.

The words *bona fide* in the previous paragraph are important since some offers are obtained by employees only as a means of forc-

---

[5] Perrin Stryker, "The Pirates of Management," *Fortune* (June, 1961), p. 170.

ing employers into paying higher salaries. The line between the ethical and unethical is very fine in this area. The ethical problem can be resolved, to a large extent, once the fairness of the employee's present salary and the sincerity of his new job offer have been determined. Actually, many such problems can be solved if recruiters inform employers of their intention of approaching an employee. When transactions are aboveboard, the possibility of a resulting free and honest agreement is increased. Unfortunately, disclosure of other job opportunities can expose employees to such retaliation as firing or refusing to give letters of recommendation. There are cases where vindictive employers have raised a salary to meet competition and fired the employee as soon as the job had been filled in the other company.

Because there are some selfish and spiteful individuals in business, it must be remembered that the principle of proportionality excuses innocent parties from exposing themselves to many risks. Young men who have come from the neat, clean world of the college may find corruption disconcerting, but business embraces men of every stamp. While candor and openness are certainly admirable qualities, the prudent man must make sure that he is not naïve. In any event, it is always well to know the men with whom one is dealing and then make a careful judgment as to what is to be done.

Despite our inability to settle all problems, we can see that several forms of piracy are unethical: that which is aimed at stealing secrets and crippling business, as well as that which leads to unlawful breach of contract or of the fiduciary relationship.

Employers who fear pirating will do well to examine both their corporate policies and their own consciences. It is not easy to lure a contented worker who is adequately paid and finds both his present work and future prospects humanly satisfying. The company that underpays an employee or does not give him a sense of growth is asking for trouble and deserves it when it comes.

BY WAY OF SUMMARY

While the concrete situation demands the consideration of a fairly large number of pertinent circumstances, the principal question remains the same: What is due to those with whom I deal? A precise notion of demands of the work contract is essential if this question is to be satisfactorily answered. The contract does not give all the answers; additional questions are necessary. Will my actions impede my independence of judgment in doing my job? Will my contemplated actions lead others to engage in unethical activities? Even if my intention is ethical, is there any proportionate reason for risking or permitting harm to outsiders such as the stockholders and the competitors of the firms with which I must deal?

7

Secrecy and Espionage

INTRODUCTION

As information becomes more and more vital in business, secrecy becomes a major ethical concern. The use of insider information, the growth of commercial espionage, and the promotion of screening methods have called attention to the problem of information control. Because nearly everyone in a company has some access to valuable information, the ethics of secrecy touches both the president of the firm and the man who empties the wastebaskets.

A secret is knowledge which a person has a right and/or an obligation to keep hidden. The most important secrets involve both a right and an obligation. These *obligatory secrets* always involve situations in which revelation of the knowledge would cause serious harm or the violation of a contract. For the purpose of analysis, we may divide these obligatory secrets into three general categories. In order of ascending significance they are:

1. The natural secret.
2. The promised secret.
3. The professional secret.

A comment on each will provide us with an analytic tool for handling some of the more common cases in business.

The *natural secret* involves knowledge of something which by its nature will cause harm if revealed. For example, an employer who knows that a worker has a criminal record realizes that the publication of this fact will make his employee's life difficult. Unless there is a *proportionate reason* for revealing the information, such knowledge is to be kept hidden. This duty of secrecy exists no matter how the information was gathered since the harm results from the revelation even when the knowledge was obtained ethically.

Generally speaking, the *promised secret* involves a natural secret. The obligation to keep it, however, arises not only from the nature of the matter, but from the promise or contract by which one binds oneself. Many business secrets are of this sort since they arise from conditions explicit or implicit in the work contract. Although such secrets are obligatory aside from the nature of the matter, they too may be revealed when silence will cause more harm than good. An employee with knowledge of the company secrets may be allowed to reveal these to save an innocent party from harm or to protect himself from an unjust accusation.

The *professional secret* involves not only an implied promise and a natural secret, but the reputation of a group whose services are necessary for society. Clergymen, doctors, lawyers, and accountants can serve society only if people feel free to give them highly confidential information. If a public accountant reveals the secrets of a client, he injures the whole system of business by reducing confidence in the profession. For this reason, only the most serious reasons can justify the revelation of a professional secret. There may even be cases where a professional man must risk personal ruin rather than violate a trust.

As noted above, any one of the secrets can be revealed when silence will cause more harm than good. This is in line with the general principles developed at the beginning of this book. Three warnings, however, are in order. First, even when a revelation is justified, it must be made in such a way as to *minimize harm*. A company physician who knows that someone has a communicable disease has to report to the proper authorities, but he is not free to tell others unless this is necessary to protect the innocent.

Secondly, we may reveal a secret to protect ourselves from a proportionate harm, but not to gain some advantage to which we have no right. Thus, I may reveal the fact that another man is a drunkard if I am being blamed for not doing work which is really his responsibility. On the other hand, I would be wrong in revealing the same fact if my only motive were the removal of a potential rival for a promotion. The phrasing, "to protect ourselves from a proportionate harm," is important, since the principle does not justify revelations for any and all causes.

Thirdly, a secret can be revealed by action as well as by word or gesture. The executive who uses insider information for personal gain has revealed a secret even though he has not even told his wife why he acted as he did.

The natural and promised secret may be ethically revealed if the person who would be harmed and/or the person who exacted the promise freely would give permission upon reasonable cause. In some cases, even the professional secret may be revealed with proper permission. Great care and discretion, however, are necessary in the revelation of the professional secret. Unless the fact of permission is known to others, confidence in the profession may still be shaken. For this reason some professionals insist that the permission be given in writing.

NON-OBLIGATORY SECRETS

There are secrets which we have *a right but not an obligation to keep*. There is *no* obligation to hide the fact that my father came from a very poor family, but I have a right to keep this to myself. If I invent a new method for making steel cheaply, I, as a private individual, am not obliged to keep this secret, but I may do so. The owner of a business may reveal his cost figures to the public if he wishes, but he is not obliged to do so under ordinary circumstances. This is merely to say that I have much *information which I may either reveal or keep secret*.

This right of secrecy is not unlimited. It may meet the claims of others and create an obligation to reveal information. Thus a seller is obliged to reveal substantial defects to a buyer. A citizen may be obliged to reveal his income to the government, although not to his neighbor. I may be obliged to reveal information whose suppression would cause grave harm to society or a large group of people. I may thus have *information which I would like to keep secret but have an obligation to reveal*, at least to some people in some situations.

Finally, there is information which I have no obligation to reveal, but which *others may rightfully seek to obtain* by ethical means. This is the case where I possess information, *but do not have a strict property right* to it. The list of my customers is something I may keep to myself, but it is also something a competitor may seek to find out providing he does not steal my papers, break into my property, and unethically violate my privacy.

Unfortunately, the line between information which I *possess* and information which I *own* is often difficult to draw. As a result, there will be areas in which it will be difficult to decide who is in the right.

INSIDER INFORMATION

By the work contract, an employee promises to keep secret information which would harm the firm if revealed. When the employee is an officer or manager, he also promises implicitly to protect the rights of stockholders for whom he is an agent or trustee. This is clearly concerned with the areas of insider information.

The use of insider information could have been treated in the chapter on the fiduciary relationship, since this relationship underlies the obligation to keep insider information inside. Much information belongs to an employee or an officer of a corporation only by virtue of his job and is to be used for the good of the corporation and not for personal profit. For example, I know that the company is about to purchase a certain piece of property. If I buy the property through a dummy and then raise the price, I have used the resources of the corporation against the corporation. I have also violated my obligation to secrecy since I revealed—to myself in my role of agent for my own interest—information entrusted to me in my role of employee. This may seem a strange way to put it, but it underlines the fact that we may often have to compartmentalize our lives if we are to be ethical.

Sometimes the use of insider information does not directly harm the company, but injures present and future stockholders. The officers of the Texas Gulf Sulphur Company who bought stock on the basis of insider information in 1964-1965 did not directly injure the company assets, although they did not help the company image. Moreover, they seem to have injured the actual and potential stockholders in several ways. They appear to have used the company information, which changed the value of stock, to exploit the ignorance of stockholders for whom they were agents. Also, by circulating false reports, they not only exploited those who actually held stock, but others who would have bought the stock barring the deception.

The use of insider information, then, can be unethical for one or more reasons. It violates the fiduciary relationship. It may injure the company and create conflicts of interest. It may injure present and future stockholders. In analyzing cases, each of these points should be considered.

CASES

In the actual world of business, even the most loyal and honest executives find themselves faced with difficult problems. A few examples will serve to illustrate the dilemmas of the honest businessman.

1. Company A has a regular policy of buying up its own stock to be listed in its accounts as Treasury stock, to be included in its pension portfolio, or to be sold to executives who have a stock option. The directors know that the value of the stock will rise dramatically when certain discoveries and innovations are announced to the public. May they authorize the company to buy up an extra large block of its own stock immediately before the announcement in order to reduce the costs to the company?

2. An executive is in charge of investing ten million dollars a year for the company's pension fund. A stockbroker who specializes in finding unlisted stock with great potential informs him that he has knowledge which indicates a certain company is a "sleeper." May the corporate executive act on this information or is he cooperating in an unethical use of insider information?

3. A stockholder, ignorant of the true value of the company, offers to sell his stock to the company treasury at a price well below its true value. The company accepts his offer. Is this an ordinary business transaction or has there been real exploitation since full disclosure of the facts might have been made?

4. A company, having discovered valuable mineral deposits in Northern Canada, offers the present owner of the land the current

market value saying nothing about the real value of the property. Is this shrewd but ethical business or exploitation?

In the first case, the company's policy of buying a certain number of shares regularly for the purposes stated need not be changed because of insider information, since the information *has not motivated* the regular purchase. However, when it decides to *increase* its purchase because of the insider information, it is taking advantage of the ignorance of its own stockholders for whom it is, after all, the agent. This is to say that the officers violate their fiduciary relationship to their own stockholders. The public use of the information is not ethical until the information is communicated to all those who have a right to it.

It should be noted that the misuse of information of this sort can injure not only present stockholders, but potential buyers, and the confidence necessary for the orderly conduct of the stock market itself. As we shall see in a later chapter, customers have rights to certain information and concealment can be unethical in many circumstances. In any event, the use of insider information involves more than injury to the firm and its owners.

In the second example, the ethical quality of the corporation's actions will depend on the answers to the following questions.

1. Did the broker obtain real insider information?
2. How did he obtain it?

It may be that the information is actually available to the public although it has not been widely diffused. In such a case, I cannot see any ethical problem, since both the broker and the pension fund officer are using a publicly available means. Often too, the knowledge or information may be the result of a shrewd deduction. For example, the broker may know that a very talented officer is about to enter the company, or he may have deduced, from public records of land purchases, that the company has made a valuable discovery. Such information is really public with the result that there is no ethical problem.

The means by which the information is obtained are often ethically significant. If any of the unethical means mentioned in previous chapters have been used, the entire operation is certainly suspect. Situations are not always quite this simple, however. The broker may have overheard something at a cocktail party, or the company may have fed him the information for its own purposes. In these cases, we must ask if the broker is obliged to keep quiet, since he is certainly not bound by any fiduciary relationship with the company in question.

In view of the various possibilities, I would venture the following tentative opinion. The company executive who is going to act on the broker's tip should not fear cooperation in the unethical use of insider information *unless he has some good reason* to suspect that the information was obtained or disclosed unethically. Even when he has founded suspicions that someone else has acted unethically without his encouragement or permission, I believe he may sometimes have a proportionate reason for using the information. There are cases where his failure to act may cost his company a great deal without protecting others from the harm.

In our third case, where the stockholder makes an offer to the company while ignorant of the true value of the stock, the directors may accept his offer in good faith if they are not free to reveal the true value of the company to all stockholders. On the other hand, if the information should be in the hands of all stockholders, they are exploiting the ignorance of this particular individual.

The fourth case, which involves the purchase of property from an owner ignorant of its true value, is different from the previous cases in two important respects. First, the company does not have a fiduciary relationship with the potential seller, as it did with its stockholders. Secondly, whereas the stockholders were in no position to get the information legitimately unless they got it from the officers, the potential seller of the land can, if he wishes to spend the money, get the same information. To put it another way, the stockholder has a right to the information because he has helped to pay for it, whereas the seller of the land has no right to information paid for by others. One might note in passing that if the company informed the landowner of the true value of the land, it would be violating its fiduciary relationship to its own stockholders.

A seller, as we shall see in a later chapter, may have an obligation to reveal certain defects to a buyer. A buyer, however, is under no obligation to reveal hidden advantages to the seller, unless of course, he is also acting as an appraiser or even as an agent for the seller as in the case when a corporation buys from its own stockholders.

In this context, it is well to note that the government is in a slightly different position when it acts as a buyer. Public officials must use their insider information for the common good of the whole of society. If the information is revealed, it must be revealed to everyone at the same time, since no group has a right to preferment in these cases. Leaking information on proposed road construction can be very unethical, since it can not only raise the prices which government must pay, but deprive owners of the value which will accrue to their property when a public announcement is made.

These few cases on insider information indicate the need for great care in analyzing the obligation of secrecy as it exists in varying relationships. In particular, attention should be given to the impacts of revelations, to the means used in getting the information, and to the rights or lack of rights of the various parties involved.

While we have used illustrative cases involving high-ranking company officials, even such humble employees as a switchboard operator may have access to valuable inside information. Indeed, a nosy and, therefore, unethical switchboard operator may be the best informed person in the firm. Secretaries too should remember that their work contract calls for secrecy; they should be on their guard against those who would seek information from them. Silence is generally golden, for both the company politicians as well as outside agents would like information which is none of their business.

OBLIGATIONS OF FORMER EMPLOYEES

The previous paragraphs apply to those who are *actually* employed by a company. Employees leave, however, and they take valuable information with them. Which of this information may they use or sell to others? Which of this information can a competitor ethically try to elicit from the former employee of a rival?[1]

A person may not use or sell information which is the *property* of a former employer without permission. To do so would be steal-

---

[1] For some other views, see Frank Chapman Sharp and Philip G. Fox, *Business Ethics* (New York, Appleton-Century-Crofts, 1937), pp. 226-229; and Burton H. Alden, et al., *Competitive Intelligence* (Watertown, Massachusetts, C. I. Associates, 1959), pp. 50-60.

ing. A person may not use or sell information which he has freely agreed not to use or sell after termination of his employment. To do so could be a violation of a contract. Other knowledge which is not the former employer's property and is not the object of a contractual agreement may be used or sold by an employee when he leaves.

These statements are clear enough, but they can be difficult to apply either because contracts are vague or because it is hard to decide when a man has a *property right* in information or knowledge.

Companies can solve some problems if there are clear and precise contractual provisions covering the use of information gained during the course of employment. If nothing else, such contracts can help the honest employee to form his own conscience. The question of a property right in an idea or information is not so easily resolved although the law of copyright and patents may provide some guide lines. Unfortunately, there are social considerations which make one hesitate in giving full ethical approval to patents and copyrights. Indeed, there may be serious doubts as to whether much business secrecy is in the interests of either consumers or the public good. For all of these reasons, I find it difficult to provide sound ethical norms for determining when an employer has a property right to ideas, knowledge, and information. Positive legal enactments may help to clarify this area, but law should consider the relationship of secrecy to the public interest.

SECRECY AND THE PUBLIC INTEREST

In general, society profits from the wide diffusion of useful knowledge. The concealment of such information and its exclusive possession tend to give some groups power over others. Modern science has made many of its advances because men felt that the results of research belonged to all members of the scientific community and ultimately to all mankind. There is good justification for such a view, since knowledge itself is a result of a social process as well as of individual efforts and brilliance. This is particularly true today when so much of our basic research is sponsored by the government or by great universities which are the agents of the general society. Even the brilliant theorist who works without laboratory and assistants builds on the research and insights of those who have gone before. In view of this, it is difficult to see how any man or group of men can claim exclusive control of any knowledge which might be socially useful.

Secrecy and the control of information may be very profitable, but the social effects of this are of questionable value. The knowledge which is buried because it might obsolete a company's present line of products robs society of real benefits. The cost figures which are kept secret may protect a company against competitors, but the secrecy may also rob society of means by which to judge the true efficiency of a firm and the fairness of its prices. The concealment of plans to relocate may save the company a long period of complaints from the community, but it may leave the community unprepared for a serious crisis. Exclusive knowledge of a new drug may help a company to recover its research costs, yet the company may be tempted to charge very high prices for an item which people really need.

All of these considerations raise questions concerning the revelation of facts traditionally held to be business secrets. Questions as to whether or not a man should have a property right in an idea are also significant here. Society may see fit to protect man in the enjoyment of the fruits of his thinking, research, and ingenuity. However, he should not be protected at the expense of society. The social interest in a wide diffusion of knowledge would seem to justify the use and sale of information belonging to a former employer in most cases where there is any doubt about the existence of a strict property right in information.

COMMERCIAL ESPIONAGE

The growth of commercial espionage and of services devoted to ferreting out business secrets bears witness to the increasing utility of information in business. It also creates ethical problems both in regard to the information which can be legitimately gathered and the methods by which it is collected.

It is stealing to buy or use information to which someone else has a strict property right, unless the owner gives his permission. It will also be unethical to hire away an employee in order to obtain information which is either the property of another or the object of a contract forbidding revelation. Much business information, of course, is covered by neither a property right nor a contract. When this is the case, the ethical problems will concern the means used rather than the information itself.

The use of bribery, theft, trespass, and fraud is unethical. Also, methods which violate privacy by the use of wire taps and similar devices are generally to be condemned. However, if we prescind from the law, which can make certain acts illegal and unethical, there may be cases where extreme measures could be justified in order to protect clear rights. These cases would be rare, since they would occur only when a businessman had good reason to suspect that a competitor was planning to use illegal or unethical means against him. To put it another way, there would have to be a situation of almost unlimited war rather than normal competition. This is to say that unjust and unethical attacks can so change the nature of competition that an honest businessman may have a proportionate reason for using extreme measures that would be unethical in ordinary, fair competition. It should be noted, however, that the ethics of self-defense or warfare demand that the attack be unjust and that all normal means of defense, such as the courts, should have been tried before extreme measures are taken. This follows from the principles of Chapter One—governing proportionality and alternate means. The law, of course, should always be consulted. Indeed, it is desirable that there be stricter laws covering the large number of gray areas that may develop.

While a large number of methods in actual use are to be condemned, there are legitimate means of gathering information about competitors. A competitor's customers are *ordinarily* not bound by any form of secrecy and are sources of valuable information about sales. The same is true of suppliers who know some vital cost figures and specifications. However, both of these may be bound by agreements, so a fiduciary relationship is not ruled out entirely.

Ordinary surveillance which does not involve fraud or trespass also seems to be acceptable. If the actions of a competitor are public enough to be observed by ordinary watchfulness, then the information gained would appear to be public. If the competitor wants to keep things secret, he must take reasonable precautions to maintain his privacy.

The terms "ordinary" and "reasonable" should cause no problem in understanding, but their application does raise difficulties. The existence of sophisticated devices which can monitor conversations through open windows or through walls with no physical trespass makes it extremely difficult, if not impossible, to protect privacy. Furthermore, because the use of such devices is becoming prevalent, there is a temptation to call them ordinary. Technological advance has created new gray areas. While the present writer is almost instinctively against the use of devices which violate privacy with or without trespass, there are many cases which can only be settled by careful legislation. In the absence of such law, companies will have to take increasing care in the protection of their secrets.

OBLIGATIONS OF THE EMPLOYER

The employer, too, has an obligation to keep secret a great deal of information about the employee. In some cases the obligation arises because the information is particularly harmful or because it was obtained under an implicit contract which limits its use. Health reports, psychological and psychiatric tests, secret investigations of the employee's credit and activities—all fall under this obligation. Even though the information was obtained ethically, it must still be used ethically. It should be kept in closed files available only to those in the company who really need the information for making decisions. Secondly, such information may not be made public without the permission of the employee. This means that the information may not be passed on to future employers or to government agencies without permission. Unethical procedures may leave the employer open to suit for a violation of privacy. The law in this area is not entirely clear, but it will probably tend to give increased protection to the individual's right to privacy and to his reputation.

JOB RECOMMENDATIONS

The principles given above may seem to pose a problem for those who must write letters of recommendations. However the problem is minimized if a distinction is made between public and private information. Public information is gained by ordinary observation of work performance, intelligence, honesty, and motivation. It is available to anyone who cares to look. Private information, on the other hand, is gained only through a confidential relationship. This information includes test results, school marks, and investigations into private matters. While an employee, in view of his position, may willingly permit the company to acquire this information, he does not make it a part of the public record. If others want this information, they too must get his permission.

Even public information which has not been widely disseminated may pose an ethical problem when some of it is potentially harmful to the employee. This may not be distributed except to individuals who have a legitimate interest in it. By legitimate interest we mean that the individual needs the information to make a proper decision about hiring or promoting a man. The fact that someone has a legitimate interest in information which is potentially harmful *does not necessarily mean that there is an obligation to provide it.* Indeed, there are cases where it should not be provided. In the first place, if the potential harm outweighs any possible good resulting from the transmission, it would seem obligatory to remain silent. In the second place, there are cases where a person can be sued for defamation because of an unfavorable letter. Prudence would dictate great caution where such a danger exists even though ethics might say there is a sufficient reason for revelation.

Although there is ordinarily no obligation to give even public information about an employee unless by his request, there is an obligation to write truthful letters once a person has volunteered or agreed to do so. A letter of recommendation that omits pertinent but unfavorable items can do considerable harm. It may not only encourage another to hire an unsuitable employee, but possibly deprive a more qualified applicant of a job. Furthermore, it can undermine confidence in the writer even though what he did say was true. Once again a thoughtful consideration of all factors is in order.

BY WAY OF SUMMARY

The present chapter is filled with references to gray areas because there are so many new problems on which there is no body of careful thought. Despite this, the principles given should cover ninety percent of the cases met in business. In every case, the decision-maker should consider the basic set of questions given in Chapter One and then use the material given in this chapter for determining proportionality. It will also be useful to check the nature and extent of the rights of all parties involved, since these rights are often either overlooked or exaggerated.

8

Honesty and
Expense Accounts

INTRODUCTION

There is much concern about dishonesty in the office and in the plant. Some estimate that petty thievery costs American business one billion dollars a year.[1] While it is impossible to document this, there are cases where the theft of small articles has amounted to hundreds of thousands of dollars in a single firm. Purchasing agents admit that in August they put in large orders for pencils, notebooks, and the like, since there is a big drain on supplies when school opens. Sometimes, the losses result from organized theft; other times the blame falls on the individual who uses the company's postage meter to mail out Christmas cards. The employee who punches another's time card and the executive who uses company maintenance staff to paint his house are equally dishonest. One way or another, theft is a serious moral and business problem.

Ethicians define theft as "taking what belongs to another when he is reasonably unwilling." Each of the key words in this definition must be understood if stealing as an ethical category is to be isolated. In the first place, the word "other" refers to both real and moral persons. While the company may seem to be an impersonal being without a face, it is a moral being with a right to its own property.

[1] Irwin Ross, "Thievery in the Plant," *Fortune* (October, 1961), p. 140.

Ultimately, moreover, theft from the company is theft from real persons such as owners, stockholders, fellow employees, and the owners of insurance companies.

Obviously there is no theft if the real owner *freely* permits me to take something. If it is his to give, his willingness transfers the title to me. The owner of a business can give regular permission for taking home small supplies and even for the private use of facilities. Sometimes the permission is explicit; sometimes it is expressed in knowing toleration of custom. The mode of expression is not important providing that the owner has signified willingness to give the item to the employee.

However, employees often see willingness where there is none. The owner or the manager may be very much opposed to "borrowing" but refrains from saying anything lest he cause discontent. In such cases, the employer's silence is not consent. Indeed, it may be seething fury in the face of theft compounded by petty blackmail. If the employee has any doubt, let him ask. If he hesitates to ask, this is a fairly clear sign that he knows that the other is unwilling.

Since being unwilling is not the same as being reasonably unwilling, the employee might ask himself what his opinion would be if roles were reversed. Neither of these methods is infallible, but they will expose much of the rationalization that is used to justify theft. At the same time, the owner is not *reasonably* unwilling if the employee is taking what is his right by contract. The typical case occurs when the employer does not pay the agreed wages, and the employee, having no way of winning a case in court, helps himself to his wages. Similar situations can occur with regard to fringe benefits and working conditions.

It should be noted that non-owner managers do not have an unlimited right to give away company property in ordinary circumstances. They, after all, are only agents. As a result, the willingness of a manager who does not have the right to alienate goods is most often not permission, but cooperation in theft. Similarly, custom should be scrutinized lest accumulated bad habits be taken as the authorization of theft. Too many people are willing to justify themselves on the grounds that it is part of the game, without realizing that the game may be crooked.

The true owner must be *reasonably unwilling* that the object be taken. Obviously it is not theft to take a gun from a madman or a child no matter how unwilling he may be. Thus, there may be objects of little or no value which the owner would not reasonably object to being taken. Even here, however, it is easy to form a false conscience. A single pencil may be worth very little, but when a large number is taken, the accumulated loss may be considerable with the result that the owner is quite reasonably unhappy about the situation.

It is often difficult to draw the line. However, because both our moral sense and the rights of others can be eroded subtly over the course of time, it is the owner who should be given the benefit of the doubt and not the would-be thief. After all, the owner does have a good title to his own goods and a congenial suspicion that he might not object strenuously does not constitute good title.

For these reasons and in the absence of permission, the use of the company meter for personal mail and the continued borrowing of pens and erasers are forms of theft. The evil is found not merely in the violation of another's rights to his own goods, but in the fact that even small thefts impair the whole fabric of trust which is one of the essential structures of both business and society in general.

OBLIGATIONS OF OWNERS AND MANAGERS

Owners and managers have serious obligations in this area. In the first place, they should set a good example lest employees, operating on the principle of what is sauce for the goose is sauce for the gander, imitate their superiors in petty theft. The double standard in this area can only encourage dishonesty. In addition, employers have an obligation to protect their goods, and they should also protect their workers from unnecessary temptation. While most people may be honest at the onset, temptation can wear resolve thin and swell the ranks of amateur thieves. It may cost money to put in a proper protective system. The money, however, is not merely an ordinary operating expense, but an investment in maintaining the integrity of the work force.

In addition, employers should be certain that their policies are forcefully articulated, since silence is often taken as consent. When theft is detected, serious consideration should be given not merely to firing, but to prosecuting in the courts. The lack of stern measures has often encouraged continued dishonesty. Worse yet, there are cases on record where employers have given recommendations to dishonest employees. Perhaps sentimentality will condone such practices. Ethics, however, must condemn them, since theft disrupts the workings of business and exposes innocent people to unnecessary losses.

EXPENSE ACCOUNTS

The much discussed question of expense accounts deals with the ethics of stealing. The fact of theft is often concealed by the absence of face to face contact and by the bookkeeping system, but stealing is stealing. Problems involving expense accounts arise from three relationships: the relationship of the recipient to the company, the relationship of the grantor to the recipient and the company, and the relationship of the recipient and the company to the tax laws.

Expense accounts can be divided into the following three general policies:
1. A flat allowance whether *annual* or *per diem* is given to the employee.
2. The employee is directly reimbursed for expenses already incurred.
3. The employee charges his expenses, and the company reimburses the seller. This form is often combined with the second.

THE FLAT ALLOWANCE

For the flat expense allowance, whether *annual* or *per diem,* the employee need not make an accounting. The allowance, however, is to be used for the good of the company. The employee who hurts the company's reputation by skimping is not fulfilling his implied contract. In some cases, the company may even intend the allowance as a hidden form of compensation so that the employee may pocket the difference between actual expenses and the flat sum.

It should be noted that this difference or residue must be reported as income, since there is still a duty to pay one's taxes.[2]

Although most cases involve an employee's abuse of an expense account, the company can also offend. Unrealistically low expense allowances can force the employee to pay for necessary and ordinary expenses out of his own pocket. If pressure is used to enforce such arrangements, there is a polite form of extortion. Careful analysis must be used in these cases for there are many legitimate arrangements whereby a company only pays part of the expenses. If this is understood by both parties from the very start and no coercion is used, there would appear to be no injustice.

REIMBURSEMENT DIRECTLY TO THE EMPLOYEE

When an employee must put in a claim for expenses actually incurred, there may be real moral problems. First, there is the problem of truthful reporting and secondly of just title to the money. The resolution of cases in both these areas depends in a large part on company policy.[3] Such policy sets forth the terms of the contract and informs the employee how he shall report and what he may claim. In general, the employee has a right and title to repayment for money legitimately spent on behalf of the company. To demand more is to take something from another who is reasonably unwilling.

Company policies generally specify that the employee should live as comfortably on the road as at home and should not suffer any monetary loss because of his work. When there is no company policy, an employee can safely follow the norm just given, since it reflects sound business and ethical thinking. Obviously this is a flexible norm whose precise content varies with the income and position of the employee. It is, nevertheless, a useful rule of thumb for both employers and employees. Of course, there are times when the

[2] On the obligation to pay taxes and its part in the ethics of expense accounts, see Thomas M. Garrett, S.J., *Ethics in Business* (New York, Sheed, 1963), pp. 87-93.

[3] For a survey of policies, see Edward F. Furash, "Problems in Review: Expense Accounts," *Harvard Business Review*, Vol. 38 (March-April, 1960).

company may want to make an impression and authorize better transportation and accommodations. This is its privilege within the limits set by the Internal Revenue Service.

Some employees are tempted to claim more than they have actually spent on the grounds that they had a right to spend more. It is argued that the company will make no objection, so long as the total bill is not too far out of line. Hence it is not stealing if the employee pockets the fruits of his own economy. This position may be justified if the practice has been explicitly approved by the proper authorities. However, two points should be kept in mind. The economy which benefits the employee does not benefit the company and may harm it. Secondly, unless the company freely makes a gift to the employee, he has no title to the money. In this type of expense account, the title arises only from the fact that money has been legitimately spent on behalf of the company.

Although the company can reimburse all legitimate expenses, it cannot claim a deduction against its taxes unless the expenditure is reasonable and necessary for the ordinary course of business. In addition, the expenditure must be substantiated in a satisfactory manner and have some definite and approximate relationship to the particular business enterprise. This is merely to say that the legal aspect must be considered in ethical problems involving expense accounts.

Because the law must be considered, certain practices which are ethical in the abstract may not be permissible in the concrete. So long as the employee has spent the total sum he claims on behalf of his firm, the sub-headings he uses in preparing his account may not be too important from an ethical point of view. However, if he reports expenses not deductible by law under headings which make them deductible, he may cause the accounting department to make illegal claims. While the I.R.S. rules demanding substantiation of claims make this less of a problem than formerly, the employee should be aware of the difficulty.

The third type of expense account, in which the employee charges his expenses and the company reimburses the seller or credit service, poses no ethical difficulties in addition to those treated, except for the problem of cooperation in theft. This question will be treated later.

DOUBLE EXPENSE ACCOUNTS

A case involving the double expense account will illustrate some of the more difficult expense account problems. A young man is invited to New York for interviews by two different companies, both of which offer to pay his expenses. The recruitee bills both companies for the full expense of the trip thus making a very nice profit. He justifies himself on the grounds that both companies were willing to pay and that if he had to make two trips, he could legitimately have made two claims. Although there is some dispute about this case, I see this as stealing, since the title to reimbursement arises not from the trip, but from the incurrence of the expenses. While an individual is entitled to have his expenses covered, he is not ordinarily supposed to make a profit.

If one of the companies makes an outright offer of payment practically in the form of a gift, the recruitee may bill the other company because he has two separate titles: the title of gift and the title of expenses legitimately incurred. I feel that the intention to make a gift should be proved rather than assumed as a ready-made excuse for lining one's pockets. Of course, the problem would not arise at all if companies asked for substantiation of all major expenses. Unfortunately, carelessness can introduce the prospective employee to temptation even before he is hired.

Similar cases can arise in advertising, public relations, and accounting firms whose representatives may be servicing more than one client on a given trip. When the problem is going to arise frequently, there is need for a policy which either prorates the expenses or assigns them on some basis—such as the primary purpose of the trip and whether or not a particular client requested the trip in the first place.

THE WIFE ON THE EXPENSE ACCOUNT

Company policies on the executive traveling with his wife vary widely. The underlying principle, however, seems to be that the company will pay for the wife when she is performing some service, since in these cases the expense is also tax deductible. Even when the expense is not tax deductible as being directly and immediately related to the good of the firm, the company can reasonably authorize such expenses on its own when long and frequent absences from home may damage the morale of the employee. It is difficult, however, to see where such expenses are tax deductible. It should be noted that, as a rule, companies grant the privilege frequently to top executives, with middle management being given the privilege only occasionally. In many cases the company will pay for the wife only when it has requested her presence.

Sometimes employees take their wives and bill the company although much of the expense was not incurred by the employee himself. This is done by taking a double room in a slightly less expensive hotel, by flying tourist instead of first class, and by eating in slightly less expensive places than when the employee travels alone. This system does not cost the company one cent extra, since the employee pays whatever expenses he and his wife incurred over his normal or allowed expenses. Despite this, the present writer feels that in the absence of approval by the company, the employee has no title to more than he actually spent on the company's behalf. Some may consider this unduly rigorous, but in an area where it is so easy to deceive oneself, it is best to stick by principle. If the employee really feels he should have his wife along despite company policy, he is always free to pay out of his own pocket.

COMPANY POLICY

The cases we have discussed indicate that good company policy can do much to help employees form sound ethical judgments and to maintain control of expenses. A good policy must conform to the tax laws, but it also must respect both the needs of the employees and the best interests of the company.

Company policy should forbid paying a man his salary through his expense account. First, if this is not forbidden, the employee may be tempted to cheat the government by not reporting his true income. Secondly, a man should be paid what he is worth directly rather than through hidden forms of compensation which may be illegal and may deceive stockholders as to true salary costs.

Company policy should forbid practices which force the employee to pay costs which should be borne by the firm. It should, in short, provide for equitable reimbursement. This involves constant updating of allowances in an economy characterized by a rising cost of living.

While the owner of a company need maintain only those controls demanded by the Internal Revenue Service, non-owner managers may have more serious obligations. Our tax laws may create the impression that the government pays for part of the expense account, but the cost to the company is real. Since the non-owner manager is handling other people's money, he should be sure that his company policy does not authorize waste. In any company, expenses should be controlled since expense accounts can be used to obtain money for bribery and other unethical practices. Sound business practice would dictate documentation and periodic audit of all expenses.

COOPERATION IN THEFT

In many cases, abuse of expense accounts and other forms of theft are possible only because of the cooperation of individuals either inside or outside the company. Thus, restaurants which supply salesmen with fictitious, inflated bills to present for reimbursement are cooperating in theft even though the restaurant gets no more than its normal return on a given sale. This is true whether the transaction is in cash or through the medium of a credit card or an ordinary charge. Similarly, the man who pads his expense account to any considerable extent suffers no repercussions from his act only because some supervisor is either careless or cooperative.

While most cases can be solved by the application of the general principles developed in the first and second chapters, a few additional warnings should be made. We must distinguish the obligation of an employee or manager—whose position puts him in charge of controlling stealing and cheating—from that of the ordinary employee. The person in charge is bound by his work contract as well as by his general obligation not to risk or permit evil. As a result, he cannot cooperate without violating his contract. It is hard to see how the principles covering a proportionate reason for permitting or risking evil can apply in his case. The supervisor who approves what he knows to be a dishonest expense account wills the violation of his fiduciary relationship. He is not merely risking or permitting the violation.

The employee who is *not* actually in charge of controlling the money or property is in a quite different position. He or she has a general obligation not to risk or permit evil without a proportionate reason, but is not bound by a contractual or fiduciary relationship. Thus, the secretary who knows that she is typing up padded expense accounts for her boss may not be able to stop the evil without losing a job that she needs. In this situation her silence is a form of cooperation, but it is not necessarily unethical.

Active and direct cooperation in which one actually wills the evil as a means to one's own advancement, is unethical in terms of the general principles we have developed. When a person benefits from the cooperation, we generally have a sign that the cooperation is active and direct and not merely a question of permitting or risking harm for a proportionate reason. This rule of thumb is not infallible and yields to the facts of the case. There are cases where the cooperation yields no monetary reward to the individual, but does make him feel that he has helped a friend. This is unethical even though no money passes hands.

There are cases where a person who is not in charge of preventing the harm may cooperate unwillingly for a proportionate reason. These are difficult cases, and even experts can disagree as to the manner of their resolution. Some, for example, feel that the restaurateur who can stay in business only if he provides salesmen with inflated bills has a proportionate reason for cooperating with them. These people reason that the man's livelihood is at stake; that he cannot prevent the evil, and that he does not will or cause the theft, but only supplies an instrument of the theft. On the other hand, it is difficult to see how he can be excused, since he lies as a means of staying in business. All would agree, of course, that the restaurateur would be unethical if he offered to cooperate or advertised his willingness through the rumor circuit. In such a case, he would be actively cooperating and perhaps initiating the evil.

Even in those fairly rare cases where a person without a fiduciary relationship might have a proportionate reason for cooperating passively, he still has a duty to work for the correction of the situation. If he refuses to do what he can, he accepts the evil and rejects alternate solutions.

In this context it should be stated that many people imagine or exaggerate the threat of harm to themselves. Their fear, cowardice, and lack of skill in handling a problem are not, however, proportionate reasons which exempt them from blame, but signs of incompetence and a weak character. Junior employees in particular are prone to use lame excuses such as the following: "The company can afford it;" "Everyone does it;" "Who am I to rock the boat?" Such excuses are indicative of a refusal to face reality and accept responsibility. In most cases, I would consider them as a fairly certain sign that the man who uses them will never succeed meaningfully in either public or private life.

PREVENTATIVE ETHICS

The employer who has the best interests of his company and workers at heart should take steps to minimize his employee's temptation to steal. An adequate company policy is the first step, but it may be useless unless higher management itself follows it. To put it another way, good example is a powerful force in any company.

Temptation can also be reduced if a worker's regular pay is adequate, relative not only to his needs, but to the importance of his position. The underpaid worker can always justify himself on the grounds that he is merely taking what is his own. Good pay thus deprives people of an easy excuse.

Although good policy, good examples, and good pay can solve the problem for most workers, the morally marginal employee will be deterred (though never completely blocked) only by adequate supervision. The regulations of the Internal Revenue Agency which demand proof of expenses beyond certain points are a great help in maintaining supervision. In addition, the internal auditors should give special attention to expenses which appear to be out of line. The mere fact that such auditing is a regular company policy will at least blunt the larcenous instincts of the moral cripple.

ADDITIONAL CASES AND
BASIC PRINCIPLES

Because there is no limit to human ingenuity and the possible situations in business, cases involving honesty and expense accounts could be cited almost indefinitely. Often these cases are presented in a nest of irrevelant detail so that basic issues are confused. Often, too, they come complete with a handy set of justifications from the employee. The honest employee will cut through these excuses and irrelevances to the basic questions.

1. To whom does the item belong?
2. Is the owner reasonably unwilling that the item pass on to you?
   a. Do I have a clear title to the item?
   b. What is the company policy?
   c. What would my opinion be, if roles were reversed?
3. In case of doubt or of unwilling cooperation with others, do I have a proportionate reason for risking or permitting the harm?

The reader may like to work through the following cases on his own. When he has finished, he may look at the questions at the end of the chapter to discover if he has overlooked any important points.

1. John is a wealthy bachelor who works only for pleasure. His employer has not paid his wages for months and refuses to do so. John does not want to bring the case to court because he enjoys working where he is and is too lazy to look for another job. He decides to take his wages by "borrowing" and padding his expense account. "After all," he says, "the wages are due to me." The employer's business is in fair condition, but his cash position is poor since he has just refurnished his offices in modern Danish style and bought a set of expensive oil paintings for the reception rooms.

2. Mary works to support a sick husband and five small children. She gets top wages, but is short of money due to heavy medical expenses. She is supposed to control all petty cash and is checked by one other employee who happens to feel sorry for Mary. By co-operating, the two manage to take about $20.00 a week with Mary getting $15.00 of this. Mary feels she has to do this, and her friend agrees for a 25 percent cut.

3. Harry is on an unlimited expense account. He is authorized to write off gambling losses with customers if he puts them down under a variety of headings such as cabs, tips, postage, etc. Harry pads all of these items even when he has no losses on the grounds that it will look suspicious if he suddenly has to put in fairly large claims for these sums. Besides, he is supposed to lose, but can't bear to do so. If he doesn't pad, they will bawl him out for not following orders.

4. Dick has been told by his immediate superior that he is not to check Miss Johnson's expense accounts. Dick knows that Miss Johnson is very friendly with his boss, and feels that there is something wrong here. The head of the entire operation is an honest man, but Dick does not want to rock the boat, so he remains silent and approves all of Miss Johnson's accounts. He's only following orders and does not know if this has been approved on higher levels.

QUESTIONS ON CASES

1. Does John have a right to the money? Even if he has a right to the money, does he have a proportionate reason for using this method before he has used the courts?
2. Would Mary's boss be reasonably unwilling for her to take the money if he knew Mary's situation at home? Does Mary's situation have any possible bearing on the actions of her friend?
3. Is Harry cheating the government or forcing the company to do so? Is there commercial espionage involved? Even aside from these questions, does Harry have any possible title to the money?
4. Has Dick neglected an alternate means? Is Dick's feeling pertinent?

IV

Relationship
of the Firm
to Other Economic Agents

9

Relations with Customers: Safety and Information

INTRODUCTION

The relationship of buyer and seller is crucial in economics, law and ethics. The way in which we view the relationship, the rules and institutions which we use to govern it, determines in a large part the success of the economic system in supplying goods and in supporting the values of society. Some view the relationship as modeled on the oriental bazaar in which the customer is a pigeon and the seller a villain. Some would like to see the relationship as a mechanical one in which natural forces take care of all ethical problems. Both views are at odds with reality and with the values of our civilization. Granted that the relationship is often impersonal, the fact remains that it is a relationship between human beings who have rights and duties. These rights and duties are the subject of the present chapter and the one which follows.

Since the relationship can take many forms, the present chapter concentrates largely on the obligation of the seller to the ultimate consumer. In Chapter Twelve, we will have something to say of the special relationship to suppliers and dealers. While the range of illustrations is fairly narrow, the principles developed can be applied in nearly all but very special buyer-seller situations.

HEALTH AND SAFETY

✓   The seller must respect the rights of buyers and users of his products. The seller may not will harm to a buyer or user as a means of making a profit. A seller may not risk or permit harm to buyers or users of his products without a proportionate reason. All of this should be obvious from the first two chapters. Moreover, these principles are the foundations of our legislation on the manufacture and sale of drugs, cosmetics, and food products. Unfortunately, our legislation does not cover all possible cases, so that it is necessary to study the application of these principles in areas not covered by law.[1]

The major difficulties in applying the principles center on the determination of what constitutes a proportionate reason for taking a risk in the absence of legislation. While there is no formula which will solve all these cases, the following points will serve to narrow the area of doubt. Even the existence of a proportionate reason does not excuse a person from attempting to minimize the risk. Thus warnings are always in order where health or safety are at stake. Furthermore, where legislation can reduce the risk by controlling the sale or use of a product, a given firm or industry almost certainly has an obligation to work for the passage of the law. This is true not only for drugs but for firearms and other lethal weapons. Quality control of the product itself may also be obligatory when risk is high. The cost of such controls is a necessary cost and not merely a means of gaining a good reputation.

Cases involving product safety are still numerous despite the existence of legislation and of increasing care on the part of businessmen. Because they can also be complex in themselves and further complicated by strong self-interest, there is probably need for additional legislation to prevent health from being sacrificed to profit. Such legislation will have many defects, since there is no such thing as a perfect piece of statutory law. Past experience,

---

[1] Court interpretations are tending to extend liability to third parties for any product reasonably certain to put life or limb in danger, even when the producer cannot be proved negligent. This theory of strict liability goes beyond ethics but must be considered by the businessman.

however, indicates that both the public and business have profited from the existing laws in this area, no matter how imperfect they may be.

In general, it may be said that the greater the danger and the larger the number of people who may be harmed, the greater the obligation to give warnings, to control sale and use to remedy the defects in the product. It should be noted that when the danger arises from cumulative use, as is the case with some dyes and food preservatives, the obligation can be effectively filled only by broad social cooperation. In other words, the fact that a given product will not harm if taken alone or in small amounts does not automatically justify the risk which results from cumulative or simultaneous use with other drugs.

THE FAIR SALES CONTRACT

Sellers must respect not only the health and safety of customers but their freedom and pocketbooks as well. Indeed, our economy depends for its justification not only on its efficiency in producing but on its ability to protect the dignity of buyers. If buyers are exploited, then we have a form of slavery in which one man is used by another no matter what label is placed on the economy. A society which permits sellers the freedom to distribute but denies the consumer true freedom is an economic dictatorship and not part of a democratic system. Historically it was the existence of such economic slavery which gave rise to communism and socialism. To the extent that such slavery exists today we can expect the increasing intervention of political power to promote true economic equality. For these reasons, the problem of the fair sales contract is of vital social importance.

Unless sellers recognize buyers as human beings rather than as enemies or as sheep to be shorn, nothing in this chapter or the following one will make much sense. It is only when we accept the dignity of the individual that we can see the ethical necessity of a fair sales contract which respects the rights of both buyer and seller.

A fair sales contract must be a free agreement. Freedom, however, must be based on knowledge. As a result, both *fraud* and *ignorance* can make a contract unfair and so unethical. Freedom also implies that the individual not only has knowledge, but is capable of acting on it. A fair contract, then, cannot be the result of *power* which forces a man to disregard his own best interests, or of *irrational desires or passion* which cause him to act as if he did not have knowledge.

In view of the nature of the fair sales contract, the seller will be unethical whenever he deliberately *uses* fraud or power, or *creates* ignorance and passion in order to gain an advantage. In all of these cases, the intent is so clearly wrong that there is little room for dispute about the ethics of such a seller. More often than not, however, the problem is not one of deliberate exploitation, but of involvement in a situation where the existing power structure, ignorance, and passion cause the buyers to agree to an unfair contract of sale. We must, then, discuss not only the more obvious unethical acts, but the more subtle obligation to remedy situations which can lead to exploitation.

FRAUD, LYING, AND DECEPTION

Fraud exists when there is a deliberate attempt to deceive someone about a material fact, that is, about a fact which has some importance for the buying decision. It is deliberate deception in a relatively serious area. Lying exists whenever one speaks against his own mind in circumstances where the other has a reasonable expectation of the truth, whether the matter be serious or not. Deception can result from fraud, lying, ignorance, or negligence, so that its ethical quality depends on more than intent.

Sound ethics condemns *not only the intent* to deceive, when the other has a reasonable expectation of the truth, but also the *risking or permitting of deception* without a proportionate reason. If I can prevent deception by expressing myself a little more clearly or by eliminating some unnecessary point which has deceptive implications, I ought to do so. At the same time, there are cases where there is no practical way of preventing the deception of some individuals. Having done my best, I cannot be accused of negligence. Of course, the greater the deception and the harm that may flow from it, the greater efforts I must make.

It should be noted that from an ethical point of view, fraud and lying can exist even though this cannot be established in a court of law. For example, television advertisers who dress announcers in white and place them in a setting which suggests a professional man's study, almost certainly intend to mislead the viewer into believing that their product has a medical endorsement. The deliberately false implication is as unethical as the outright lie even though it may not be as effective in deceiving the public. The same implication might be ethical if it were indeliberate or could not be removed without removing some truthful statement which gave important information about the product.

In dealing with the proportionate reason required to permit or risk deception, it is important to consider the basis for the act and the nature of the audience. Thus, the honest advertiser need not bother himself too much when the deception results from the buyer's carelessness in reading properly printed instructions or from his wishful thinking. At the same time, the advertiser should realize that the courts, which formerly judged a statement deceptive if it would fool a reasonably prudent man, are beginning to look to the protection of even the gullible and the ignorant. Both ethics and the trend in law, then, would dictate the use of reasonable care in protecting nearly everyone from possible deception.

In attempting to evaluate the deception which might possibly result from a statement or implication, the advertiser should keep his audience in mind. Terms and usage which may be clear to those in the industry or to professional buyers can often be confusing to the ordinary consumer. Indeed, I have found an executive who had not the slightest idea of the meaning of the promotional terms used by his own salesmen. The confusion of someone about to purchase this man's product must be great. Industry cooperation with the Federal Trade Commission has done much to remedy this problem in some industries, but there are still numerous sectors where the language is clear only to the seller.

Sellers often object to agreeing to standardized terminology and grades which make it easier for the consumer to compare values. To a certain extent their objections are based on the fact that such standardization may make it difficult to promote either marginal differences or real innovations which were not foreseen by the standard maker. Such difficulties are real and should be anticipated. However, they should not cause one to overlook the buyer's need for information. I suspect that often the real objection is not quite so reasonable, but rather stems from the fear that standards would enable the consumer to see through the partially fictitious values of branded and heavily advertised goods. If this is the case, then, industry may be using its power to prevent the consumer from getting the most for his money.

IGNORANCE AND DISCLOSURE

Both ethics and law agree that the seller has an obligation to disclose latent material defects to the buyer if there is to be a valid contract. Except in the case of the genuine as-is sale, the seller does not have a proportionate reason for allowing the buyer to remain in ignorance of such defects. There is, however, a problem as to what constitutes a latent defect in our modern economy. Thus, while a defect is generally considered latent if ordinary inspection will not reveal it, modern packaging and processing often make inspection difficult if not impossible. Moreover, when the buyer is faced with thousands of items in a supermarket, he does not have the time to make even an ordinary inspection. As a result, consumers often find themselves practically unable to get even necessary information. Because the producer and seller are in a position to provide information and because the information is necessary for truly informed buying, I believe that there is an obligation to reveal not only latent defects in the strict sense of the term, but many ordinary defects and even positive qualities.

Obviously the right of the consumer to information is not unlimited. If good product information is readily and cheaply available to the user, he cannot ask the producer to supply it as a matter of duty. To put it another way, the consumer must take reasonable steps to remedy his own ignorance before the producer has an obligation to reveal more than latent substantial defects.

DISCLOSURE IN THE SALE OF CREDIT

There are few areas where full disclosure is more important than in selling credit. Because figures puzzle many people, even simple compound interest can cause such confusion that people are deceived. When discounts, service charges, and varying methods of repayment are introduced, it takes a determined and sophisticated borrower to ascertain the true cost of the money he is buying. Most people never think that the insurance they pay to cover payment of the loan in case of death or disability is a cost. In addition, there is considerable and expensive ignorance about alternate and cheaper sources of credit, with the result that there is more than a little exploitation in our economy.

If anyone thinks this is exaggerated, let him ask his friends and a few fellow workers to compute the true annual percentage cost of money in the following cases.[2]

1. In a revolving credit plan, the customer pays 1½ percent on the unpaid balance at the end of the month. What true annual interest is he paying for an item bought on the 29th of June, when he pays $1.50 interest on June 30th for $100.00?

2. A teacher's credit union charges a contributing member $1.50 interest a month on a loan of $100.00. In figuring, don't forget that the member has some of his own money in the fund from which he is borrowing.

Honest credit agencies do try to disclose the true cost of borrowing. For some reason, however, large groups fight legislation that would require such disclosure. It would almost seem as if they want to profit from the ignorance of buyers. This opposition to reasonable measures of preventing exploitation is as unethical as the exploitation itself, since it involves the use of power to continue a harmful situation that need not exist to the same degree.

Realistically, it must be admitted that some people cannot be taught or do not want to know the true cost of credit. The obligation, then, is to use reasonable means and not any and all means.

When there is an obligation to reveal defects and positive qualities, this may be done in a variety of ways. In some cases, it is the job of the salesman; in others, the task falls to labeling and advertising. Traditionally, of course, it was the salesman himself who had the duty of informing the consumer. However, with the growth of impersonal selling through machines and self-service racks, and with the increased number of salesmen who are really only order takers, it would seem more and more necessary to give information on la-

----

2 For case material, see Hillel Black, *Buy Now, Pay Later* (New York, Morrow, 1961).

bels and in advertisements, even though these are not technically offers to sell. At the same time, the space and time limits of labels and advertisements reduce the obligations to the consumer, since only the most pertinent information can be given in many cases. Often, too, the advertisement is designed to call attention to the existence and availability of the product, so that it cannot be made to bear full responsibility for informing the public.

SOME SPECIAL PROBLEMS IN ADVERTISING

The advent of television has posed some interesting technical problems for the advertiser who wants to be truthful. Some products do not photograph well, with the result that a television picture of the actual product would be deceptive and useless as advertising. In view of this problem, producers of television commercials use a variety of techniques to assure a true picture of the product as it actually is. Hot wine is often used in place of steaming coffee, and blue shirts must sometimes be used instead of white. In short, the object actually photographed is changed so that the picture will represent the true product. When such procedures are necessary in order to present the truth, it is hard to agree with those government agencies which label the practices deceptive. At the same time, if the technique is used to enhance the appearance of the actual product or to denigrate the product of a competitor, deception is involved in varying degrees. The use of toothpaste for shaving cream in an underwater scene is deceptive unless the shaving cream could have passed the identical test. The norm is always whether or not the picture presented deceives the viewer as to the true nature of the product. After all, even a skilled speaker must exaggerate his intonations in order to convey his ideas. Similar license should be allowed to others so long as the final impression communicated is a truthful one.

While it would be impossible to give a long list of specific problems and practices in advertising, the material prepared by the Better Business Bureau and the Federal Trade Commission will be both more up to date and more detailed than anything given here.

Two practices, however, need special comment since they are sometimes confused with legitimate selling tools. In particular, it is necessary to distinguish preticketing from legitimate markdowns, and "bait and switch" advertising from the "loss leader."

Preticketing, or the manufacturer's placing a retail price tag on his product, is legitimate in the abstract. In the concrete, however, it is often a form of cooperation in deceptive pricing and advertising. Some manufacturers use inflated suggestive retail prices so that sellers can convince the buyer that he is getting a real bargain when the price on the tag is dramatically marked down. The product is not meant to sell at the inflated price, and the preticketing is not meant to inform, but to deceive by establishing a fictitious basis of comparison. Such procedures harm not only the consumer, but honest competitors, so that they are doubly unethical.

The legitimate markdown is a reduction in price based on either the normal or actual selling price in a store or area. It is not deceptive because the basis of comparison is real and not fictitious. Some markdowns are difficult to classify from an ethical point of view except in terms of the seller's intention. A merchant buys some dresses at a particularly low price and wants to sell them as a special. Because this particular merchandise is unfamiliar in his market, he believes customers will not realize what a bargain they are getting unless he displays the markdown. He puts the dresses on sale at what would be their normal price in other markets and in a few days marks them down to the price he actually wanted to charge. Since he does not intend to deceive, but to inform of the true value, I would adjudge his intention and act as ethical in the absence of laws to the contrary. If his intention had been to deceive as to the normal price, his act would have been unethical.

The "bait and switch" advertiser promotes a fictitious bargain which he does not intend to sell and generally does not stock in any reasonable quantity. He uses the promise of a bargain to bring in the customer whom he then tries to switch to the high priced merchandise he actually intends to move. If the customer insists on the promised bargain, the merchandise sometimes is brought out and discovered to be no bargain at all. More often the buyer is told that the item has already been sold out. Such tactics have been widely used by shady appliance dealers and home improvement companies to the detriment of both consumers and honest competitors. It is false advertising by intention and effect and has done much to harm and lessen public confidence in many retailers.

The "loss leader" is a product sold at a loss in the hope that the customers attracted by a *real* bargain will buy enough other merchandise to yield a good profit. In the absence of laws to the contrary, the "loss leader" is ethical so long as the seller has a reasonable stock or informs the public of the limits of his stock. It is not a deceptive practice, though it can be suspect if other products are given an extra mark-up in order to insure the profit. In many states there are, of course, laws governing sales below cost, and these should be studied carefully lest what is ethical in itself be illegal in a given area.[3] Conflicts, indeed, are very possible, since the law often looks to the protection of the competitor rather than to the benefit of the consumer.

IRRATIONAL DESIRE

The critics of business accuse it of encouraging people to live beyond their means. Some businessmen affected by these charges suffer pangs of conscience when they see people buying things they cannot afford. So long as the businessman has not deliberately encouraged buyers to act irrationally, he need only make reasonable efforts to help his customer act intelligently. In most cases these efforts would amount to no more than pointing out those elements of the situation which the customer may have overlooked. Often indeed, there is nothing to be done since people resent meddling even when they are not deaf to unpleasant facts. There are cases, however, where stronger action may be required.

Funeral Directors are generally dealing with people whose emotions make them incapable of rational choice. Guilt-ridden, hypnotized by the awful present, the survivors will often neglect their own future. Their inability to cope with facts, figures, and the future makes them profitable customers for the "friendly" mortician. Here is a case where the funeral director must look not only to his pocketbook but to the needs of the living. If he does not, he can be *a*

<hr>

[3] Morton J. Simon, *The Law for Advertising and Marketing* (New York, Norton, 1956), pp. 396-401.

cause *if not the* cause for leaving a widow with nothing but receipted funeral bills.

Similar situations arise with the young couple buying an engagement ring, parents arranging a wedding, and people borrowing money to pay for medical expenses. To a lesser extent many salesmen exploit the emotions of parents in peddling encyclopedias to people who cannot afford them. I have seen a new set of a prominent encyclopedia in the home of poor Puerto Ricans who could neither speak nor read English and had to use a cardboard box as a crib for their baby. It is difficult to label this anything but exploitation of ignorance and passion. While the businessman is not the financial advisor of such people, he must still take reasonable measures to make sure that he does not exploit emotion and irrational desire.

The extreme cases given above should not be taken to imply a condemnation of emotion.[4] Our feelings can support us and help us to focus our attention. Sellers and advertisers can use emotion to help consumers. What we are condemning is the exploitation of people whose emotions, uncontrolled by reason, cause them to act irrationally.

Our examples are drawn from personal selling rather than from advertising since the real crisis exists in the realm of face to face contacts. Elsewhere, we have shown that advertising itself is probably a marginal factor in producing irrational behavior based on emotion.[5] To be sure, the intention to exploit through appeal to emotions is unethical, but the harmful effects of much advertising can be offset by the good effects when the advertiser is not seeking to distract from the objective facts.

PUBLICITY AND PUBLIC RELATIONS

The shared responsibility of producer, agent, and media is nowhere so apparent as in publicity and public relations. While an advertisement is a paid announcement and recognizable as

---

[4] See Thomas M. Garrett, *An Introduction to Some Ethical Problems of Modern American Advertising* (Rome, Italy, Gregorian University Press, 1961), pp. 37-52.

[5] *Ibid.*, pp. 95-132.

such, publicity and public relations stories appear as unbiased editorial material. For this reason, all who are involved in processing or publishing such releases must be extremely careful. This is especially true in financial public relations where a lie or a false implication can cause serious financial harm. No financial editor wants to find himself touting stocks on the unexamined information of a public relations department, nor does a reputable P.R. man wish to be duped by some unscrupulous executive. Wishes are not enough protection, however, and competent checking is in order.

Product publicity which appears in the shopper's guide poses the same sort of problems. Often there can be potential conflicts of interests when a hungry advertising department pressures the editorial people to do them a favor by giving a free "plug" to an advertiser. The editorial department needs to be insulated from such pressure and indoctrinated with the idea that it must guard the consumer rather than the ad salesman's commissions.

The shared responsibility of many agents in the advertising, public relations, and publicity processes points up a more general problem in business ethics. Whenever responsibility is not assigned with some precision, it tends to evaporate into a cloud of excuses. In such a cloud, not only self-regulation, but any regulation becomes an impossibility or, at best, an accidental occurrence. Good ethics demands that such situations be avoided since they are a breeding ground for unethical or at least irresponsible conduct. In the case of advertising and public relations, it should be made clear that although one man must ultimately take the praise or blame, each agent is responsible for reporting errors he may detect. Moreover, it is generally necessary to specify who must check for accuracy when copy is passed from one independent group to another.[6] The television networks, for example, make their own check of medical claims made by advertisers and have located the responsibility clearly in their Continuity Acceptance Departments. The other media and local stations would do well to imitate them in this, although, of course, their resources are more limited.

[6] The courts are beginning to recognize the liability of all agents. Cf. "Kastor Hilton is Fined $50,000 for Regimen Ad Role," *Advertising Age* (June 28, 1965), pp. 1 and 8.

PACKAGING AND LABELING

A package has numerous functions. It protects the product in transit and in storage; facilitates use; provides information about the contents; and in many cases, serves as an advertising medium. Unfortunately, a package can be defective in the performance of any one of these functions and may even be used to deceive consumers.

Most of the ethical problems, however, do not involve the use of packaging for outright deception but the failure of the package to give adequate information. In most cases, the problem is closely connected with the manner and method of advertising itself.

There is the problem of the "large economy size" that actually costs more per ounce than the regular size, the "cents off" sale in which no information is given about the regular price, the use of odd ounces, the reduction of contents without reducing package size, the slack fill, and the use of small type for essential information. Most of these problems can be solved by asking the following questions based on our principles.

1. Is the package intended to deceive or exploit?
2. If there is no intention to deceive, is there a proportionate reason for permitting or risking deception?

Proportionate reasons may exist in this area when one function of the package demands that another function be neglected in part. The slack fill is often a result not of the intention to deceive, but of the nature of the product itself which settles in transit. A small package may demand small type. Providing a handle on a bottle may produce a shape which does not reflect the true contents or size. The utility of having a standard package size in a given line may justify the odd ounce content, since obviously space is not directly related to weight.

On the other hand, there are many practices which are actually deceptive, no matter what the intentions of the packer. There can be absolutely no excuse for calling a package a "large economy size" when it actually costs more per ounce than the regular size. It is difficult to imagine any proportionate reason for the introduction of such descriptive terms as "tall," "giant," and especially "super quart." Such terminology is either misleading or meaningless. It is hard to see anything but deception when a roll-on deodorant in a plastic container is then put in a box twice as large as is required. It is difficult to see any justification for using small print and poor contrasting backgrounds on a package which has plenty of room for the senseless illustration which is already on it.

Possibly the most potentially deceptive practices are found where a packager reduces the contents without giving any prominence to the statement of contents. The danger is compounded when the package is then labeled "2¢ off," although the new price per ounce is actually higher than the old one. Of course the consumer can frequently detect some of these frauds if he comes armed with a slide rule, computer, and a photographic memory which has recorded all the previous prices. However, even this highly sophisticated equipment will be of little help if the housewife is surrounded by six screaming children.

The 50th National Conference on Weights and Measures is working towards model regulations for packaging. By making standards uniform, they would help not only the consumer, but the packager who at present must cope with conflicting state regulations.[7] The National Conference ruling provides not only definitions of the "principal display panel" and a table of type sizes, but requires definite color contrast, generally horizontal placement, and a free space around the quantity statement. The packaging industry believes the provisions are reasonable and workable. Certainly they are an attempt to eliminate many practices for which there is no reasonable excuse.

Existing legislation forbids abuses in packaging, and more legislation is probably needed.[8] Unfortunately, some of the proposed laws are less reasonable than the suggestions of the National Conference on Weights and Measures or the demands of sound ethics. I believe that great care is needed in setting up standard definitions of allotments and standard package sizes for everything. At the same time, it is possible to work out flexible standards on fill and change of weight and content. Some companies already use double labeling

[7] "Who Needs the Hart Bill?" *Modern Packaging*, Vol. 38 (January, 1965), pp. 83-87 and 174-180.

[8] For a brief summary of existing laws, see "Legal, Safe and Nondeceptive," *Modern Packaging Encyclopedia* (New York, Modern Packaging, 1965), pp. 64-74.

which indicates not only the price of a given package, but the price per pound or ounce. A company can also standardize its own packaging in such a way as to make maximum use of shelf space, warehouses, and trucking. The results will be increased profits along with lower prices to consumers. Granted that there are difficulties which demand caution, the fact remains that cooperation in this area could improve the efficiency of our distribution sector.

Mere self-interest should move American packers towards standardization. In the absence of standards it is difficult to enter into agreements with the increasing number of nations that do have them. As a result, exporters may meet growing difficulties in foreign markets. The retailer, of course, has much to gain if he can make better use of his space even though individual manufacturers may lose the marginal advantages they gain from some oddity in their packaging. In short, it will pay to rationalize another sector of the economy.

THE ETHICS OF BUYERS

The ethics of buyers is to a large extent the reverse side of the ethics of sellers. The buyer too must not exploit by fraud or power or passion. His position with regard to ignorance, however, is slightly different from that of the seller. The seller must disclose substantial defects to the buyer, but with a few exceptions, the buyer does not have to reveal hidden virtues to the seller. The assumption is that the seller, having the property in his own hands, should know its worth.

While sellers must disclose substantial defects, this does not excuse buyers from gathering information and comparing products. The buyer, after all, has an obligation to use his resources intelligently. Often, indeed, it is the careless buyer who has made it possible for the dishonest seller to deceive and exploit ignorance. Industrial buyers who are skilled can help to improve economic performance, but lazy consumers who buy without information can encourage the substitution of tricks for real value. The shrewder that buyers become, the easier it will be to enforce honesty in the market place. If buyers are skilled, honesty will not only be good ethics, but the best road to profits.

There are a few cases where the buyer, being also the appraiser, may be obliged to reveal hidden values to the seller. The jeweler who is asked the worth of a diamond by an owner who wishes to sell, should either suggest a separate appraisal or state the true value in trade at that level. If the jeweler answers by making an offer well below true value, he may be using his role as an appraiser to help himself to an unfair profit in his role as buyer.

BY WAY OF SUMMARY

The seller is unethical whenever he intends to exploit whether he causes the deception, ignorance, and passion, or deliberately sets out to take advantage of it. In other cases, where the seller is not the cause of the buyer's disability and does not intend to take advantage of it, he may proceed if he cannot change the situation by reasonable means.

In the following chapter, we shall meet problems involving the use of power to exploit. In Chapter Eleven we shall consider some side effects of unethical exploitation of consumers, and in Chapter Twelve, we shall return to study relationships of dealers and suppliers.

10

Relations with Customers: Prices

INTRODUCTION

Prices and the price level affect the welfare of sellers, buyers, and competitors as well as the functioning of the competitive system and the economy. As a result, the fairness of prices is a central issue in business ethics as it is in law and economics. At the same time, it is a difficult question for which there is at present no completely satisfactory answer in either theory or practice. At times pricing practices give the appearance of competition, but in reality only protect sellers at the expense of consumers. Prices which are most beneficial to consumers and individual sellers can lead to economic concentration and possible government control. Laws designed to protect small dealers can and do raise prices and subsidize inefficiency. Indeed, the laws often encourage pricing which reduces efficiency and robs the economy of even the limited benefits of competition.

In many cases it is nearly impossible to evaluate the long-range effects of prices, for our economy is so dynamic and complex that uncertainty can be high. The variety of buyer-seller relations makes generalizations especially dangerous. Existing theory can further confuse our perception of the reality of pricing, for it often rests on false assumptions. It is no wonder, then, that businessmen are uneasy, critics outraged, and students of ethics frankly puzzled. We are indeed in much the same position as we were when treating wages; convinced that there is a norm, we are unable to pin it down with satisfactory clarity. Once again, then, we shall proceed cautiously, pointing out obvious abuses and giving some broad rules that will at least narrow the gray areas.

DIFFICULTIES WITH EXISTING THEORIES

Older theories of the ethics of pricing suffer from two defects; they are inapplicable to many segments of the American economy and they make no allowance for the cost of price instability. These defects arise from the fact that both our economic and ethical theory were developed to explain or regulate a much simpler economy. Even though these older theories may not be very useful today, a brief consideration of them will help to illustrate the problems involved in any theory of fair pricing.

In simpler economies characterized by near perfect competition, prices were set by the *collective judgment* of a fairly large number of buyers and sellers. So long as there was real freedom, it could be assumed that the resulting price, or rather range of prices, was fair since it represented a community judgment of the *exchange value* of the goods in question. Resources were also allocated in accord with the value judgments of the community, since the prices tended to equalize supply and demand. In this way, both individual justice and the social good were served. It was with such a market in mind that medieval writers and their followers equated the fair price with the free market price. The price or *price range* so established was binding on both buyers and sellers unless some particular circumstance, though never the need of the individual buyer, justified a lowering or raising of the price.

This theory which corresponds closely to the classical economic model of price formation is inapplicable to large segments of our economy since the market is not perfect, and large buyers and sellers are often in a position to set the price unilaterally within broad limits. Buyers, moreover, often lack the information necessary to form correct judgments of exchange value. The problem arises from the fact that the present market does not equalize the power of buyers and sellers, but tends in many cases to build up power blocks which can call the tune. For all of these reasons the theory which equates the fair price with the free market price is not too useful in an economy where many markets are not truly free.

Some might assume that we could change the economy in such a way that free markets and fair prices would prevail once again. This change would not only be impossible, but might not produce the desired social results.[1] While true price competition certainly gives consumers lower prices and the economy fair prices, it also tends to produce instability which makes it difficult to plan research, innovations, and future markets. It is for this reason that many companies avoid price competition and seek to administer prices in the interest of stability and planned growth. It is for the same reason that governments have frequently intervened to fix prices either directly or indirectly. In short, the cost of the perfect market may be too high for the good of society and large groups of individuals. To put it another way, the prices set by perfect competition may not maximize even economic welfare in the long run.

It should be noted in this context that price instability can be particularly hard on individuals and institutions which depend for their income on savings, investments, and pensions with a fixed value, but not a fixed purchasing power. Moreover, although drops in prices may benefit the poor, raises can be disasterous for many groups. A glance at the curse of the depression or run-away inflation will confirm most of these statements.

DIFFICULTIES WITH THE LAW

Even if the businessman wanted to engage in real price competition, the law would often prevent him or at least moderate his enthusiasm if his efforts proved profitable. If General Motors priced its products to assure the maximum total profit, it would so undercut its competitors that there would soon not even be the semblance of competition. At this point General Motors would find

[1] For a survey of economic thought on the question, see William Lee Baldwin, *Antitrust and the Changing Corporation* (Durham, North Carolina, Duke University Press, 1961).

itself faced with an anti-trust suit. As a result, General Motors, like so many leaders in fields where there are few competitors, finds it safer, if not more profitable, to hold back and permit other companies to stay in business. This provides us with the appearance of competition, but not with its classical virtues. It also gives us a set of administered prices and an ethical problem.

The Robinson-Patman Act, Fair Trade Laws (which are actually resale price maintenance laws), and the laws on sales below cost can reduce price competition while preserving the appearances of it.[2] We are, then, faced with a paradox. The laws, which should bring the benefits of competition in price to the consumer, actually discourage price competition. Indeed, the final result may be the creation of a situation in which the businessman cannot enter into truly fair contracts of sale even if he desires to do so. In any event, the law often creates proportionate reasons for risking or permitting the undesirable effects of many pricing practices.

PRICING PRACTICES AND PROBLEMS

Because power is a fact and the law encourages it indirectly, prices are not set by competition in large segments of the economy. More often than not, they do not result from a free interchange between buyers and sellers, but are set in a variety of ways and in view of a variety of goals. This is true not only of the prices of commodities and finished products, but of labor. To a certain extent, it must be this way. The new product has to be offered at some price, and if there are no substitutes, the seller may have wide latitude since buyers, having little basis of comparison, may be willing to accept it. Moreover, many businesses can survive only if they charge for future costs and future services in the price of products they are selling here and now. This, of course, brings in the whole problem of capital formation in the modern American economy. It raises questions not only of the fairness of prices but of social utility when private groups such as the modern corporation are allowed to be major instruments of capital formation through their ability to exact a sort of *forced savings* from the customer.

[2] B. S. Yamey, *Economics of Resale Price Maintenance* (London, Pitman & Sons, 1954), especially pp. 108-117 and 129-130.

A VERY TENTATIVE THEORY

Our remarks thus far should indicate the difficulty of evolving a modern ethic of pricing which is adequate to the economy as it exists. Indeed, I do not believe that our understanding of the economy and its relationship with the political order is great enough to permit the development of an adequate theory at this time. In the meantime, it is suggested that a rough judgment of the fairness of prices can be made in terms of the four factors which can vitiate the fair sales contract; *fraud, ignorance, power and passion.* As in the past chapter, allowances must be made for the existence of proportionate reasons for permitting the unwilled effects of some acts and situations which cannot be easily changed. This, of course, leaves many of the broader social questions untouched. We shall, however, return to them in our chapter on the relationship of business to the social economy.

PRICE FIXING

Conspiratorial price fixing is condemned not only by the law but by ethics. The reason is that the *conspiracy causes power to destroy equality between buyer and seller.* Furthermore, it involves a type of fraud since the buyer is led to believe that he is dealing with independent offers. When the price fixing results in actual losses to the buyer, we are, in addition, dealing with a type of theft or at least unjustified damnification. Finally, conspiratorial price fixing interferes with the economic mechanism which is supposed to govern the pricing and distribution of products.

Conspiratorial price fixing tends to exist in industries with certain common characteristics: overcapacity, special buyer specifications, and buyer power—at least to postpone purchases, if not to demand price concessions.[3] In such industries, real price competition can destroy or cripple smaller and less efficient operators just as it is supposed to do in classical theory. Unfortunately, real price competition can also lead to anti-trust prosecution of the survivor and to

[3] Clarence C. Walton and Frederick W. Cleveland, Jr., *Corporations on Trial: The Electrical Cases* (Belmont, California, Wadsworth, 1964), pp. 11-28.

waste of resources which are sunk costs and cannot easily be applied to other uses. Strong producers and even society thus have some interest in protecting marginal producers. Conspiracy is, nevertheless, both an unethical and illegal method of attaining this goal. Furthermore, because inefficiency is protected, the whole of society has an interest in deciding how the situation should be remedied. When private groups decide, they are really usurping authority which society has not given to them.

PRICE LEADERSHIP

Legally, price leadership is not the same as price fixing. The effects, however, are often identical. In particular, power makes customers pay more than they would in a truly free market. This means that they are "taxed" to assure the continued existence of marginal firms as well as to increase profits of efficient producers. The evil of price leadership, moreover, generally results from the fear that the leader will use its power to retaliate against those who dare engage in price competition. Once again, it is power which causes the destruction of true economic freedom for both producer and consumer.

Given the actual situation in many industries, it is difficult to accuse either price leaders or followers of unethical conduct without qualification.[4] Does a particular company have any real choice about following or leading? Even if it has a choice, can it exercise it without inviting retaliation from either competitors or the government? The answer to these questions will sometimes indicate that a producer may have little or no freedom to change the existing practices. In short, there comes a point where it is the entire complex rather than the isolated acts of individuals which creates exploitation through power. When this is the case, a producer who does not intend to produce these effects may permit them for a proportionate reason. Often the reason is simply that he can do nothing to provide an immediate remedy. However, the producer must recognize the existence of an obligation to work for a remedy in the long run.

[4] Martin L. Bell, "Ethics in Oligopoly Pricing Practice," in Joseph W. Towle, *Ethics and Standards in American Business* (Boston, Houghton Mifflin, 1964), pp. 197-209.

When such situations exist, justice or at least an approximation of it can be restored only by society as a whole. There is a price to pay for government intervention, but the price must be weighed against the costs already being incurred. This is not the place to settle the issue, but it should be clear that the solution will not be found in slogans but only in careful research and the imaginative development of new economic systems. While no solution will ever be perfect, we must admit that we have been fairly successful in devising systems which regulate utilities in the interests of consumers, while preserving many of the benefits of private enterprise. Perhaps, the scale necessary for many industries will indicate that time is creating new natural monopolies which cannot and should not be controlled by the market, but by the society as a whole.

THE ADMINISTERED PRICE

We must face the fact that producers do not want price competition in many cases. Price competition disciplines the inefficient and limits management's freedom to plan for the future. As a result, the administered price is an ideal which firms would like to make a reality since it gives them more freedom and greater stability. While the administered price takes several forms, at base it is a price set by producers and sellers rather than by the forces of short run supply and demand. The price, usually decided by the principal producer or supplier in a given line, is more stable than prices set by supply and demand, so that planning is more feasible. Moreover, since it is generally followed by competitors, buyers have little choice. It is not a monopoly price since both competitive forces and the fear of government are always present to some extent. However, many firms are well enough insulated against the full impact of a free market and so can control their profits and prices within fairly broad limits. The result is that customers pay more for the product than they would in a free market. The power position of the company brings this about.

However, it is not easy to condemn the administered price out of hand. Some firms which enjoy this privileged position use the extra margin of profit for research and expansion. It may be argued that the consumer pays less in the long run. In addition, part of the price may be considered an investment by the consumer in the future of the economy. While such investment is certainly a social necessity, we may ask whether or not it is healthy for private firms to have so much say about the allocation of resources against the future. In point of fact, they actually have the power to tax or to force savings which is ordinarily reserved to the government. Furthermore, because they are at least partially free from the competitive pressure of the financial market, they are no longer completely responsible to even this limited social control of resources. We are then faced with a problem which deserves serious study from both an economic and ethical point of view.

While this is not the place to discuss the full social and political significance of administered prices, the businessman should not dismiss the problem lightly.[5] Administered prices allow many companies to accumulate capital, power, and the possibility of controlling larger and larger areas of the economy, not by virtue of real productive and distributive efficiency, but because of their financial position. Sooner or later the existence of such power which is not directly controlled by society will call forth more and more government regulation. This day can be postponed by public relations and lobbying, but in the long run, society cannot permit large private power centers which are not responsible to the best interests of society. If the market no longer demands accountability and no longer enforces the discipline which promotes fairness by equalizing power, some other agency will be found.

I do not believe public opinion can do the job completely, for public opinion is not an entirely independent or directed force. Neither do I put much faith in the theory of countervailing power which entails one giant holding another in check. Power can neutralize power selectively so that the powerless and the unorganized —consumers, for example—are still exploited.

Because of the legal situation and the actual structure of industries, society as well as business must bear the blame for the situation. Unfortunately, law and existing systems are not easily changed so that the obligation is not to cease administering prices at once,

---

[5] Gardiner C. Means, *The Corporate Revolution in America: Economic Reality vs. Economic Theory* (Crowell-Collier, 1962), gives possibly the best insight into the significance of the administered price.

but rather to seek a solution in which all interested parties play a part.

Actually, an adequate solution is impossible except within the larger framework of the American economy. Companies with administered prices often pay the best wages because they are able to do so. Pure price competition may rob us of this benefit, yet there is the suspicion that these adequate wages result from a power struggle between big companies and big unions in which the consumer ultimately pays the bill. We cannot, then, attain the power balance necessary for a just society without considering the power of unions as well as that of corporations.

RESALE PRICE MAINTENANCE

While our laws forbid horizontal price fixing (that between competitors), they sometimes permit and even encourage vertical price fixing (that between producers and their dealers). While these laws are given such euphemistic labels as "Fair Trade Laws" and "Quality Stabilisation Laws," they serve to reduce price competition and force higher prices on consumers. Like conspiratorial horizontal price fixing, resale price maintenance practices also serve to protect marginal and inefficient economic units by guaranteeing them higher margins of profit than they could obtain in real competition.

Obviously someone benefits from resale price maintenance, but the question is whether the benefits offset the losses and whether the benefits are gained by unethical means.

The manufacturer of branded items wants resale price maintenance to protect his product image from erosion resulting from its use as a "loss leader" or as a heavily discounted item. If one or more merchants continually sells his products with a low mark up, the manufacturer fears that customers will refuse to pay more. Retailers who face this type of competition are liable to follow suit and ask the manufacturer to reduce his price. When large discounters are in the field, the manufacturer has to deal with several powerful buyers who can hurt him or at least reduce his freedom. All in all, then, resale price maintenance helps the manufacturer shelter himself from some of the forces of the market. His desire to do so is understandable when he has spent large sums on advertising and branding. His acts, however, may not improve the performance of the economy and the lot of the consumer in any significant way.

Resale price maintenance protects the dealer from competition. However, it also restricts those who consider their profit a result of volume rather than of a high mark-up. This means that the consumer cannot benefit from all the economies of scale in selling. Further, by discouraging low price and volume selling, resale price maintenance protects dealers who for one reason or another have not reached or do not want to reach the most efficient scale of operations. The manufacturer is not unhappy about this since his channels of distribution are protected, but the consumer must pay more.

Sometimes it is argued that price margins must be kept high in order to insure service. Consumers, however, do not always want to buy service, and resale price maintenance forces them to purchase more of a package than they desire. Here is the use of power to force prices up or at least to make consumers buy more than they want. This, in our opinion, is unethical. The power of government is being used to protect the interests of one private group at the expense of another private group in circumstances *where this is not necessarily for the public good.* Indeed, I believe it is against the public good, insofar as this is generally understood, to include creating the maximum freedom in business consistent with good order in society as a whole.

Fortunately, large retailers and discounters have an interest in removing resale price maintenance laws from the books, so that in many cases the public has had some freedom of choice. Others, however, continue to seek the passage and enforcement of these laws which tax the consumer without returning proportionate benefits to the society as a whole. This group, it seems, believes in freedom for producers but not for buyers and sellers who want to serve those customers interested in price.

PRICE AND ADVERTISING

False and misleading advertising certainly leads to unfair prices since the customer pays more than he would have if he had known the truth about the product. This is one of the major reasons for condemning false advertising as unethical. Even technically honest advertising can create illusions which lead the consumer to pay more than he should. This is not the fault of the advertiser alone, but of careless buyers who identify the branded and advertised item with quality and sometimes even use price as an index of quality. In most cases, of course, advertised and branded products are of good quality, readily available, and carefully controlled. Price differentials, however, reflect more than the costs needed to provide these services. Thus a physician who prescribes drugs by their generic name rather than by brand name saves his patient a bit of money. The shopper who buys private unadvertised labels of the great merchandising chains such as Penney's can often get superior merchandise at prices below those of advertised brands of similar quality. Often, the private label is made by the same company to the same specifications, the difference being in the buyer's illusion rather than in any quality of the goods. Each case, however, should be considered on its own merits, since facts take precedence over theory. When the facts are known, the principles can be applied.

It is difficult to draw the line between true value and actual price. It is also nearly impossible to conceive of a method by which even the most scrupulous advertiser can avoid creating some illusion. So long as buyers are careless, there is little an advertiser can do. As long as competition takes the form of advertising and nonprice differentation, it would be suicide for many manufacturers to change their tactics. In addition, it must be admitted that even if all buyers were very efficient, we would still need advertising to inform and persuade rationally. In view of this, it seems to me that the real ethical problem arises when producers and retailers use fraud and power to prevent those who want price differences from enjoying them. In particular, the use of resale price maintenance laws appear unjust in this context.

The above paragraphs are not to be taken as an approval of the deliberate attempt to get higher prices by creating an illusion. They are, rather, a recognition of the limits of the producer's power to avoid harm and of the proportionate reasons for permitting what is almost inevitable in a society composed of fallible human beings. Once again, the ethics of the businessman is enmeshed in the whole web of human society so that it cannot be governed by an ethic designed for angels.

PRICE AND PASSION

An unjust price can result not only from fraud and power, but from passion and irrational desire which can destroy or limit freedom. The most obvious example, as mentioned previously in Chapter Nine, is that of the case of the funeral director who can sell the bereaved almost anything at any price because the person's emotions have robbed him of rationality and control. There are times, of course, when even the honest funeral director cannot dissuade the survivors from a foolish act, but there would seem to be no excuse for charging inflated prices no matter how foolish the customer.

Something similar can be said of loan companies who are dealing with people either in dire straits or so hypnotized by desire that they lose all sense of proportion. We do not mean that the businessman is his customer's conscience, but he does have an obligation to use reasonable means to prevent another human being from harming himself. In the case of the loan company, this at least involves some effort to inform the customer about the true price of the money he is borrowing.

In recent times, advertisers and sellers have been accused not merely of exploiting existing passion, but of creating it for their own purposes. The intention to create an irrational passion which can be exploited is objectively unethical. However, it is very difficult to say whether or not sellers can create this passion with any ease or consistency. Thus, advertising for all its effectiveness is only a marginal force in creating demand. Furthermore, in a great many cases, its effect on demand increases rather than decreases rationality. As a result, each case is to be examined on its own merits rather than included in a blanket condemnation of persuasive advertising. Where there is no intention to create and exploit irrational desire, the seller's obligation is only to take reasonable steps to protect the customer from stupidity.

While there may not be a great many cases where passion is either created or exploited, these do exist and should not be overlooked. The ticket scalper and the person who initiates scare buying, are both in this class. Their price and their profit are not a result of fair exchange, but of exploited inequality. Actually, there are two evils here: the harm to rationality and the unnecessary dent in the customer's pocketbook.

In certain areas, price is so much higher than cost, even though one is dealing with volume sales, that passion, power, and fraud all seem to be involved. In particular, this is true of toiletries and proprietary drugs. In these cases, unfortunately, much of the difficulty is the fault of the consumer who wants to be fooled or is so emotionally involved that he refuses to use his head. In short, the customer is a sitting duck asking to be shot and then seemingly enjoying it. For example, there are people who take price as a certain sign of quality and will not buy the less expensive item even when it is the best available. As a result, sellers resort to double and triple pricing for the same product, since only thus can they cover all segments of the market. Although this situation results in people paying more for the product than it is worth, it is difficult to condemn the individual seller. However, the cumulative effects of this may cause serious misallocation of resources in society, so that the situation itself is an evil. Whether or not this calls for legislation, that is, control by society as a whole, will depend on the severity of the harm. We must face the fact that every society must tolerate some evils lest the remedy be worse than the disease.

DISCRIMINATORY PRICING

As we saw in the chapter on hiring and firing, discrimination is unethical only when based on factors which are not relevant to job qualifications. The case of discrimination in pricing is similar but more difficult, since it is not always clear what factors are relevant in pricing. In addition, discriminatory and unethical pricing injures not only buyers but competitors as well. Finally, it can even be difficult to determine what constitutes the mere fact of a price difference since there are a vast variety of discounts, allowances, fees, services, and premiums which certainly affect the cost to the buyer. A trade-in allowance may be a real reduction in price, but under some circumstances it can conceal a price increase. Discounts given to employees may be actual reductions in price or increases in wages depending on one's point of view. Rather than become involved in unnecessary subtlety, we shall treat price as the actual money cost to the buyer and allow disputed points to be settled by the conscience of the agents involved.

Everyone will agree that the cost of manufacturing for shipping to and servicing a buyer is relevant to price differentials. All other things being equal, it costs less to process and ship large orders. A seller is not discriminating against those who buy in small lots when he passes on part of the savings to a big buyer, so long as the reduction is available to all who can meet the cost-related conditions. At the same time, so long as the price is fair, there is nothing in ethics or law which forces the seller to pass on all or part of the economies of scale.

The cost justification of price differentials is unfortunately complicated by the Robinson-Patman Act and its enforcement. Many of the problems arise from the fact that the seller must justify his reductions. This is easier said than done, for costing is neither an exact science nor an art whose rules are accepted by everyone. As Fennelly has pointed out, the businessman may use one method of justification while lawyers and the courts use another.[6] The result is that it is often difficult to tell when one is violating the law even if a particular price is completely ethical in the abstract.

Because it is difficult to assign costs, sound ethics demands not mathematical precision, but an honest effort. At best, even the most honest businessman can only make a rough estimate. As Fennelly has noted,

> To a business manager, for example, the cost that can be attributed directly to one business transaction is generally less significant than the average cost of one or a large number of similar transactions and the cost of doing business with one customer is much less significant than the average cost of doing business with a large number of customers. [7]

Because neither business nor accounting is really set up to take account of the actual costs of a given sale, it may be impossible if not unreliable and misleading to try to determine such a cost with mathematical precision.

---

[6] Donald J. Fennelly, "On the Judging of Mince Pies," *Harvard Business Review*, Vol. 42 (November-December, 1964), p. 82.
[7] *Ibid.*, p. 77.

Although the law may not always recognize them as legal, discounts given to promote good will or win word of mouth advertising appear to be ethical even though the precise benefit to the seller cannot be calculated. In this class are discounts to professors, clergymen, and others whose opinion is highly respected. Discounts to employees, if not treated as part of their wages, may also fall into this classification. If nothing else, custom would seem to tolerate these differentials.

Other discriminations have traditionally been justified on the basis of the buyer's need rather than on the seller's cost or advantage. Discounts to charitable institutions and some nonprofit organizations are generally acceptable, probably because the recipients are not in competition and thus not subject to our ideas of the ordinary commercial relationship.

Both laws and ethics recognize the legitimacy of price differentials needed to meet competition. Once again, however, the law's requirements are such that honest businessmen cannot always tell when they are acting legally.[8] This exception merely recognizes the fact that the seller can in the face of competition have some proportionate reason for risking or permitting harm to the competitors of those who get a more favorable price.

Functional discounts paid to a buyer who performs a service for the seller, such as warehousing or brokering, are also ethical and legal since they really reflect a cost differential to the seller. Problems, however, arise when it comes to determining the size of the discount since it is difficult to cost these services.

Not only the seller but the buyer is bound by the ethics of price discrimination. Big buyers are often in a position to extort concessions that are not related to their own efficiency or to the cost savings realized by the seller. Often, too, the seller wants to give price concessions to big buyers. The reason, underlying all volume selling, is that a smaller unit profit means little if volume gives a much greater total profit. Indeed, if a seller has unused capacity or idle equipment, a discount that wipes out all unit profit, but helps him to cover overhead and fixed costs may be very good business. Whether the concession is extorted or given freely because it is truly profitable

---

[8] It has been extremely difficult to use the need of meeting competition as a defence. See Heinrich Kronstein, John T. Miller and Ivo E. Schwartz, *Modern American Antitrust Law* (New York, Oceana, 1958), pp. 119-127.

for the seller, it can hurt competitors of both buyer and seller. If the hurt results from objective factors like efficiency or cost savings to the seller, then there is nothing unethical about it.

Since the profit of the seller is not necessarily an indication of cost savings, it is not a justification for discrimination in itself. Both law and ethics permit discrimination when it is necessary to meet *bona fide* prices of competitors, but once again the interpretation of the law makes it difficult to defend oneself on this ground.

As we have noted several times, the Robinson-Patman Act complicates ethics at this point since it makes it difficult, even impossible, to defend an action for price discrimination. Indeed, it often leaves businessmen in doubt as to whether or not they are violating the law. Some refer to this as the law which it is impossible to obey. Others say it is not a question of obeying the law, but of deciding which of its provisions you will break since you cannot simultaneously observe all even with the best good will in the world. In the concrete, the law which was designed to prevent real abuses has often led to an abandonment of price competition, since this has become almost inherently dangerous. As a result, the law may protect competitors, but it may actually lead to consumers' paying more. We would venture the opinion that there is need for much reworking of our legislation in this area.

BY WAY OF SUMMARY

In the practical order, the businessman must ask himself whether he has obtained his price as a result of free agreements which protect the legitimate interests of all, or whether his profits represent the result of power, fraud, ignorance, and passion. In many cases, he will have proportionate reasons for permitting or risking harm that he cannot prevent or cannot mitigate at any reasonable cost. Finally, because he is an important part of society, he may have an obligation to work for the elimination of situations which provide excuses for giving less than perfect justice.

Because competition is not an unmixed blessing and private power potentially if not actually unjust, the establishment of prices which are both fair and socially acceptable will demand study and action beyond the direct control of business.

11

Relations with Competitors

INTRODUCTION

The ethics of a businessman's relations with his competitors is not identical with the ethics of competition, which includes the study of the effect of acts on the competitive system itself. It is quite possible for an act to be fair and just to competitors and yet so injure the system that the government forbids the action by law. Unfortunately, our laws are not always clear as to whether competition, competitors, or the consuming public should have first place. Indeed, as we saw in the previous chapter, some laws protect the appearance of competition at the expense of the public. Moreover, there are increasing doubts as to the value of competition in many sectors of the economy. In the present chapter we shall concentrate on relations with competitors rather than on the system itself. As a result, our conclusions always bear the qualification, explicit or implicit: *unless this be unethical because of its social effects.*

GENERAL PRINCIPLES

A competitor is ordinarily not an enemy but a rival. As a result, relations with competitors should be governed by basic ethics and the rules of fair play rather than by the ethics of self-defense and warfare. Unfortunately, an unethical competitor can turn rivalry into a ruthless battle. Therefore, there are cases where, *all legal remedies having been exhausted,* the ethics of self-defense comes into play. In the present chapter we do not treat these cases, but assume that competitors are ethical and engaged in business rather than in jungle warfare.

As in every other sphere it will be unethical to will a major harm to a competitor whether as a means or as an end. As in every game, however, not all can win. The ethical businessman may often have a proportionate reason for permitting or risking harm to a competitor. Thus, if I win away my competitor's customers by offering truly superior service and low prices based on volume savings, I am hardly unethical. After all, the economy exists ultimately for the consumer and should reward those who do the best job, unless efficiency is unethical because of its social impacts.

Because of the linkage between sellers and consumers, practically every practice which is unfair to consumers is also unfair to competitors, since it takes away business by means other than product, terms and service. Fraudulent advertising, for example, not only bilks the buyer, but robs a competitor of business to which he was entitled on the merits of his product. In the present chapter, we shall not reconsider all the cases taken up previously, but concentrate to a large extent on those cases where the competitor is the primary victim.

DENIGRATION OF COMPETITORS

It is obviously wrong to lie about one's competitors or their products. The unfounded whispering campaign which tells of insects found consistently in soft drinks and the false rumor that a competitor's product contains harmful substances fall under this condemnation. It is not so easy to decide cases when the harm results from *truthful and founded* statements. The difficulty resides in the fact that even the truth, as we said in the chapter on secrecy, can sometimes cause more harm than good. The truth, indeed, can be a two-edged sword that cuts the user as well as the intended victim. Perhaps a competitor does use inferior materials, but the revelation of the fact may cast suspicion on the entire industry. To put it another way, the man who throws mud must be on his guard lest some of it be blown back by the wind. On the other hand, silence can also be unethical if it exposes others to unnecessary harm. Each case must be carefully judged on its own merits. In general, the businessman may and sometimes must make truthful though harmful statements about competitors in the following circumstances:

1. To prevent a competitor from cheating or harming a consumer.
2. To stop a competitor from using unfair practices. For example, I may warn a consumer that the competitor's product has not held up well in use, or I may point out that he is engaging in deceptive advertising.

Despite these exceptions, the good of the business community generally demands that truthful if disparaging statements be made in private or if possible to trade associations or law enforcement groups who have a legitimate concern. In particular, disparaging advertising should generally be avoided since its public nature may tend to lower confidence in an entire industry and not merely in the competitor. It is for this reason that most advertising groups are against comparative advertising.

A distinction should be made between disparagement by direct statements and disparagement by implication, since nearly every positive satement about the worth of one's own product implies in some way that the competing products are not as good. If product X is the best or the most economical in fact, others must in some way be inferior. The implication is such an accepted part of American advertising that no one bothers about it, although such comparisons are forbidden by the law of other nations. When the comparison is effectively meaningless, there is certainly no great ethical problem. In other cases, the implication may be harmful or false or both. An advertisement which puts all of its stress on the safety of electrical heating might imply that other forms are unsafe. If the statement of fact is true, the ethics of the implication are to be judged by the rule given above. It would seem to the writer, however, that it would require less of a reason to permit harm from the implication of the truth than from a directly disparaging truthful statement. The reason is simple. If one were required to avoid all damaging implications, it would soon be impossible to say anything significant.

UNFAIR INTERFERENCE AND
RELATED PRACTICES

It is possible to harm a competitor by interfering with his production and distribution. Thus at one time unethical competitors helped foment labor disputes and work stoppages as well as boycotts of a competitor's products. Such crude and clearly immoral practices are not too common today, but there are still cases involving the hiring away of key employees or the use of market power to move the competitor's products into a corner, if not off the shelf, in retail establishments. Our problem is to draw the line between unfair interference and legitimate competitive practices. Indeed, the problem is not, as a rule, in the fact of the interference, but in the method used to produce it. The key question is generally whether or not the interference results from providing more efficient service or from the intention to harm the competitor.

Hiring a competitor's workers as a means of harassment and of crippling his operation is unethical. Hiring his workers as a means of enlarging and improving one's own operation is both good business and good ethics. The ultimate effects on the competitor may be the same, but the intention plus the potential benefits to consumers makes the difference. We assume, of course, that there was no breach of contract or of fiduciary relationships.

Employees should beware of job offers that contain conditions relating to the revelation of trade secrets. Not only is there the danger of cooperation in theft, but also of personal loss. Experience shows that that those who are dishonest in one area are dishonest in others. As noted in Chapter Seven, it is not always easy to draw the line between trade secrets and other information gained in the course of employment. However, integrity demands that an honest effort be made to distinguish cases and assure fairness to all.

In competing for shelf space in retail establishments, a salesman is generally ethical so long as he gets favored spots on the basis of his product or legitimate service to the storekeeper. Better design, packaging, displays, price, advertising supports, and delivery are all part of the service. Unfair competition enters with extortion, bribery, kickbacks, and the granting of discriminatory advertising allowances or brokerage fees. In these areas, the Robinson-Patman Act should be consulted since many of these practices are covered by law as well as by ethics.[1] Those who want to complete the catalogue of unethical acts in this area should refer back to Chapter Ten and look ahead to our treatment of relations with dealers in Chapter Twelve.

A few practices are difficult to analyze since the harm to a competitor is offset by benefits to the consumer. Merchants, for example, are indignant when a competitor advertises a price reduction on a specific nationally advertised product which is "fair traded." Such a practice hurts, but may also help consumers to get information about real bargains. The advertising may be unethical if it breaks a real contract or violates a just law, but it cannot be condemned merely because it hurts a competitor. This brings us to the difficult question of price cutting.

PRICE CUTTING

Price competition is supposed to be the heart of the market economy. Yet, price cutting is a dirty word because so many men fear price competition and dream of price stability. As Bunting has pointed out, there is a schizophrenic attitude here.[2] Moreover, it is an attitude which complicates ethical analysis by substituting slogans and epithets for thinking.

Like most questions in the present chapter, the ethics of price cutting is a question of intention and means and not merely of effects on a given competitor. Indeed, price cuts are, in general, a legitimate and desirable competitive tool whose harmful side effects on competitors are offset by the benefits to consumers and the economy as a whole. In the ideal world of the perfect market, price cutting would be the most ethical way of competing. The reason is that in such a never-never world, no one seller could really hurt anyone. In the real world, however, price cuts backed by power can be used as a club to obtain advantages that have nothing to do with quality or service to the consumer.

---

[1] Wright Patman, *Complete Guide to the Robinson-Patman Act* (Englewood Cliffs, New Jersey, Prentice-Hall, 1963), pp. 102-147.

[2] John R. Bunting, *The Hidden Face of Free Enterprise* (New York, McGraw-Hill, 1964), pp. 58-59 and passim.

In the concrete, we condemn price cutting which is *intended* to harm a competitor. This is particularly reprehensible when the ultimate aim is the establishment of a power which can be used to exploit customers. A test for the presence of such unethical intentions is found in the question: "Is this price cut calculated to help the business without exploiting consumers either now or in the future?"

Undercost selling is often, but not necessarily, a sign of the unethical intention mentioned above. A company may ethically sell under cost to liquidate inventory which is tying up capital. It may ethically use "loss leaders" as a promotion so long as its general price level covers expenses. Often it may be necessary and ethical to sell below cost in an effort to recoup at least some fixed costs in hard times. All of these price cuts may hurt competitors, but they are ethical, since they are not purposely aimed at either harming competitors or at exploiting present or future buyers.

The ethics in this area are complicated by the existence of laws on sales below cost in some thirty states. Since these often forbid sales below cost because they might tend to create a monopoly or divert trade or even lessen competition, they cover more actions than our principles in the present chapter. The exceptions allowed in these laws are also allowed in ethics, so that they can provide a catalogue of proportionate reasons. Simon lists the following exceptions in *The Law of Advertising and Marketing*:[3] a *bona fide* clearance sale advertised as such; sales of perishable merchandise to forestall loss; imperfect or damaged merchandise sold as such; discontinued merchandise sold as such; a final liquidation; sales for charitable purposes and to relief agencies; sales to government; sales made in good faith to meet competition; sales by court order; sales to employees of tools and the like used in the trade. Not all exceptions hold in all states, nor do all exceptions in ethics apply in law. As a result, it is necessary to know the local regulations.

What has just been said can be applied to almost all industries characterized by an approximation to real competition. The careful student of ethics, however, will see that there are situations where additional factors must be considered. The following cases will indicate some of the problems that the ethical businessman must face in this area.

[3] Morton J. Simon, *The Law of Advertising and Marketing* (New York, Norton, 1956), pp. 397 ff.

1. A building contractor in bad financial condition makes a very low bid on a job in order to recoup some of his fixed costs, keep his staff, and stay in business for a while longer. When the demand for buildings is low and the number of builders high, such a situation may become common. They can also be disastrous for the industry. In the first place, such bidding may make buyers unwilling to pay prices which allow a reasonable profit. In the second place, it may tempt builders to conspire to rig bids in order to protect themselves. In the third place, the desperate builder may go bankrupt in the course of fulfilling his contract and leave the job unfinished. Finally, there is a temptation to cut corners, substitute lower grade materials, and otherwise violate the contract in order to break even.[4]

The desperate bidder we have described may intend to fulfill the contract according to specifications and so have a completely ethical intention. Does he, however, have a proportionate reason for running all the risks we have described? In most cases, the bidder has not caused the situation. Often too, his failure to bid low will not remedy the situation. His bid may be below cost or close to it, but it is a reasonable means of cutting loss and staying in business. By every ordinary criterion, he seems to have a proportionate reason for making his offer, yet risks remain.

Actually, we are dealing with one of those situations where competition as a fairly orderly process has broken down. The obvious solutions, moreover, are either forbidden by law or repugnant to many businessmen. The problem could be solved by the industry's setting up standards and qualifications, but this would look like a conspiracy in restraint of trade. Indeed, it could very easily become just that. The second solution would involve the use of law to enforce strict bonding requirements or to forbid bids below cost. Such a law, of course, would create problems about entry into the business and involve more supervision than many would like.

This type of problem illustrates the need for broad industry and social cooperation which considers the impacts of both business and legislation on many groups. The fact that isolated individuals are relatively powerless to prevent the evil creates an obligation to work for such broad control as will minimize the harmful effects.

2. The owner of a small but efficient firm with unused capacity

4 Cameron O. Hall, ed., *On-The-Job Ethics* (New York, National Council of Churches of Christ in the U.S.A., 1963), pp. 31-35.

wants to lower prices in order to increase volume and profits. He has, of course, every right to do so. Indeed, it is in the interest of the public. He fears, however, that larger though less efficient firms will retaliate by cutting prices even below cost and so nullify his attempt to improve his business.

The producer in question is certainly justified in not cutting prices in such a situation. His larger competitors have not made any actual threat, in which case they would be guilty of extortion, but the effects are such that these harmful results follow; a competitor is robbed of legitimate freedom and the public is deprived of the benefits of price cuts. On the face of it we have a real evil without anyone committing a clearly unethical act. This is a result of the fact that real power works even when it is not used. It deters even if its possessor does not actually threaten to use it. Once again we are faced with a problem of competition that cannot be solved by the individual conscience, but requires broad social cooperation and legislation.

3. A large and efficient company could make a greater profit with lowered prices and increased volume. The owner is in no danger of retaliation and indeed will probably drive his smaller and less efficient competitors out of business. Such a course of action, however, would attract the attention of the anti-trust watchdogs and possibly lead to annoying suits. As a result he administers prices and protects his less efficient competitors. In the end, the public pays more for products than it should and would in a truly competitive economy. Once again no one has performed a clearly unethical act, but the evil results. Once again the solution can only be found by changing the laws and extending our understanding of the good in true competition. All too often we have maintained the appearance of competition while suffering from the evils of monopoly. Until such changes are made it is difficult to accuse of an unethical act the businessman who does not compete on price.

These cases should indicate that the ethical problems concerning the relationships of competitors cannot be considered aside from the relationship to consumers. In addition, they should show the necessity of supplementing individual ethical decisions by legal measures designed to assure that there is sufficient social cooperation to prevent or mitigate harmful effects which cannot be controlled by individuals.

COOPERATION AMONG
COMPETITORS

Although our anti-trust law forbids cooperation which is detrimental to consumers or the economy as a whole there are large areas in business where cooperation is in the best interests of all parties in the economic process. To a certain extent, trade associations are expressions of the need for cooperation. Unfortunately, many trade associations are purely defensive organizations and do not exhibit a creative approach to common problems. Despite this, the general obligation to operate one's business efficiently in the service of the consumer would seem to demand that businessmen look to greater cooperation within the existing legal framework. There are even some areas where they should work to change the framework so that they may better serve the public. The airlines which cooperate by sharing information on maintenance, safety, and passenger handling have found each of them profits from this procedure. Similarly, many small grocers have found that their very survival depends on cooperative buying and advertising. There are many other areas where cooperation may be the clue to future progress. We may ask the following questions: Is secrecy necessary in all research projects? Could cooperation here limit waste? Would not cooperative limitation of advertising for products with a stable global demand increase everyone's profits? Are there not areas in which standardized terminology and packaging could reduce shipping and marketing costs without crippling imagination and initiative?

Some firms are coming to realize that cooperation by licensing patents may also be beneficial at the same time that it helps the public. It is even possible that a wide sharing of all sorts of information would actually increase everyone's profits without harming the public. Here and now, we do wish to take a definite stand on any of these questions. It is suggested, however, that there may be real positive obligations in this area—obligations which arise from concern for the good of the company as well as for the legitimate interests of consumers.

UNETHICAL COOPERATION AND COMPETITION

Illegal and/or unethical cooperation, whether it be conspiracy or an informal imitative venture, exists when competitors combine not in the interests of real productive and distributive efficiency, but in order to exploit the weakness of buyers by power and fraud. While the main point has been developed sufficiently in the previous chapter, some of the underlying causes of such unethical cooperation are pertinent to a consideration of relations with competitors.

No seller really likes the true competitive process which will discipline him if he fails or slackens his efforts. This is particularly true if there is a buyer's market or sporadic demand. In addition, if the seller has high fixed costs, real price competition can easily turn profits into losses. As a result, such sellers want to insulate themselves from price competition and uncertainty. When this is done by deceiving buyers or cooperating against them, we have unethical conduct.

While the means used to insulate oneself from competition are unethical in many cases, we must face the fact that in some cases the businessman is trying to avoid some evils which can harm not only the company, but the industry and even the public. We may then condemn the means and still sympathize with some of the goals of these businessmen.

Competition which leads to monopoly may rob the public of even the limited benefits of oligopoly. Thus real monopoly will demand government control of prices and frequently stop the benefits of such non-price competition as innovation, quality control, and better service. Whether the benefits of one system outweigh the benefits of another is a moot question. It is certain, however, that sellers do not have a right to make a unilateral decision and then enforce it by unethical means. Some are interested in price, and they should be able to negotiate a free purchase untrammeled by fraud or coercion. It may be that many industries should be monopolies controlled in the public interest. This decision, however, can only be made by the society as a whole and not by private individuals.

Competition which leads to chaotic price changes certainly does not benefit company, industry, and most buyers. However, the decision as to whether or not the value of stability outweighs the values of competition should not be unilateral and unethically enforced. Sound values and the ideals of our economy demand that both buyer and seller participate in negotiating truly free contracts of sale and purchase.

In the great electrical price fixing conspiracy, the companies certainly thought that they were asking a fair price. However, the fact remains that the investigation of their activities began when TVA had a foreign bid which was some 6 million dollars lower than the lowest bid made by one of the conspirators. A bid of 12 million as opposed to a bid of 18 million leaves one with some doubt about the objectivity of the conspirators' judgment of fairness. Moreover, the TVA pointed out that the low bid of the Parsons Company of England could not be explained merely on the basis of labor costs which were only 1.5 million less and then offset by import duties.[5] This would seem to indicate that unilateral decisions of fairness can be very lopsided. It may also indicate that the industry is overexpanded and less than efficient. Both of these causes often lead to unethical conduct.

THE MORAL ATMOSPHERE OF COMPETITION

The ethics of competition cannot be divorced from the ethics of relations with workers, suppliers, stockholders, customers, and society as a whole. For this reason, nearly every chapter in this book has something to do with the ethical problems arising from the relations with competitors. It must be repeated, therefore, that the attitude towards competition and business itself will be a controlling factor in the application of the principles developed to cover all of these areas.

If competition is viewed as a form of warfare in which the object is not to serve the consumer, but to destroy the competitor, we can expect a steady disintegration of standards. In war, after all, no

[5] Clarence C. Walton and Frederick W. Cleveland, *Corporations on Trial: The Electric Cases* (Belmont, California, Wadsworth, 1964), pp. 30 ff.

weapon has been banned until obsolete, and every practice has been justified in some way on the grounds of survival. While competition is not by nature a warfare, but rather a race to serve the public, there are cases where an unfair competitor turns the game into a battle. Where the law offers no remedy, the temptation is strong to retaliate in kind and to meet force and trickery with force and trickery.

The truly ethical businessman must resist the temptation lest he find that he has won a battle and lost the war. Unethical retaliation for unethical attack destroys confidence in business and introduces chaos where order should reign. It substitutes tricks for real competence and leads to a weakening of all human ideals. The correct solution is not unethical retaliation, but an effort to unite the industry behind true ideals and to secure such legal regulation as is necessary to protect the honest merchant. Only in this way can a man protect his soul as well as his business.

When conspiracy, theft and bribery become the pattern in an industry, costs are forced up and honesty, even within companies, is diminished. The increased costs often lead to a decrease in quality and services with the result that business is less efficient in serving the public. I know of one country where advertisers blackmailed their advertising agencies into kickbacks until the agencies ended up doing little more than passing on orders for space in newspapers. When this situation became widespread, the development of advertising techniques and services was paralyzed with the result that the distribution system, already poor, stagnated.

It should be recalled that a competitor's tactics are not unethical merely because they pinch. To prove unethical conduct, you must show either that the intention is evil or that the competitor is permitting harm with no proportionate reason. Perhaps the average human being cannot make such distinctions when he feels that he is the victim. However, unless such distinctions and allowances are made, competition can degenerate into total war.

For all of these reasons, business must recognize that it often needs an outside referee and that government can be the friend of the honest businessman even though there is a price to pay.

12

Stockholders, Dealers, and Suppliers

INTRODUCTION

In the good old days when businesses were managed by their owners and firms did not tower over their suppliers and dealers, the world of business ethics was considerably simpler. In those days a man could look out for his own interests within the limits set by the fairly clear rights of others. Even in the days of industrial capitalism when the manager worked for a tightly held corporation or family business, a man still knew to whom he was responsible and for what. Today, however, we live in a world of collective capitalism where managers are the employees of a corporation whose legal owners are so numerous as to form a faceless mob, and so powerless as individuals that they often have little control over what is technically their own property. On top of this, the manager of the giant collective enterprise has power over the lives and destiny not only of his own workers, but over less powerful firms which may depend on his company in a special way. The existence of this power over suppliers and dealers plus a changing relationship to stockholders, creates special ethical problems for the manager of the large corporation. The problems are the more difficult, since we are not always sure of what the relationship is or what significance it has for others.

In an earlier chapter, we solved several ethical problems by considering the manager as the agent of the corporation and of its stockholders. Although the manager is certainly this, he is a great deal more in many cases. He is, at least in the case of the large corporations, the mediator of the overlapping if not conflicting interests of investors, workers, dealers, suppliers, the local community, and the national economy. He is at once an executive, legislator, and supreme court justice. He has not, however, been elected by those whose interests he must reconcile. Often he has not even been chosen in any significant sense by the stockholders. Within limits, he is frequently not accountable to anyone but his peers in the managerial aristocracy. Like any human being, the manager of such a corporation must anticipate reactions to his decisions and fear retaliation by other economic agents, if not by the government, but he has more freedom and often more power than elected representatives in the government. More often than not, he has little fear of being put out of his job once he has reached the top. The top executive may not always appreciate his freedom and power, for he is acutely aware of the union, his competitors, and the government. If he has any sensitivity, he is also aware of the obstacles which exist within his own organization. For all of this, he enjoys considerable freedom and power without, in most cases, having any formal constitution to guide him in his use of it. Perhaps it would be most accurate to say that he has wide discretionary power for which he is ordinarily answerable largely to himself or to a few of his peers.

The situation we are describing is neither an accident nor the result of deliberate comprehensive planning. It evolved as businessmen and society made a series of adjustments to constantly changing needs. For a long time, most people were not even aware of the cumulative effect of the changes so that they still spoke in terms of an ethic which no longer covered all the duties and responsibilties of management. Now, however, increasing attention is being given to the actual state of affairs and to the development of norms of behavior which will apply to the new world of business. In a process of adapting and changing, the norms may not always be satisfactory. Yet, as has been noted several times before, the attempt to isolate problems and develop principles is a vital necessity.

RELATIONS WITH STOCKHOLDERS

Although the stockholder is legally the owner of the company, his legal claims against it are minimal. There are some legal remedies, but the stockholder's ability to use them are limited by his ignorance and by the cost of initiating and sustaining a suit against a group with vast resources. Actually, most stockholders do not appear interested in exerting any control over their company so long as it is profitable either in terms of dividends or the increasing value of its stock. This is reflected in the attitude of management which often sees its first loyalty to the company itself rather than to the stockholders. The manager realizes that the stockholder must be served in some way, but this is not necessarily his chief concern. This is as it should be, for other claimants on the corporation have more urgent needs and make greater contributions to the corporation. This fact needs to be stressed lest the ethics of the manager be unduly narrowed. As Berle has pointed out,[1] the stockholder does not, as a rule, invest in the corporation, but in the stock quotation. In the case of new stocks and bonds, the buyer is a real investor in the sense that he adds to the store of capital, but ordinary stock purchases do not allocate capital so much as they redistribute liquid claims. Thus, in the vast majority of cases, the stockholder does not supply capital and often does not take much risk. Indeed, if it were not for legal limitations, the more prosperous companies could buy up all of their own stock and finance most of their operations and expansions out of retained earnings, bond issues, or loans from banks. In such a case, the corporation would own itself, and we would no longer have the fiction of private ownership.[2]

All of this does not mean that the stockholder has no rights, but that they are not as clear and simple as some would lead us to believe. Furthermore, even though it may not allocate capital very often, the stock market is necessary for the performance of other

---

[1] Adolph A. Berle, *The American Economic Republic* (New York, Harcourt, Brace & World, 1963), pp. 129 ff.

[2] See this worked out by Andrew Hacker in his introduction to *The Corporation Take-Over* (New York, Harper & Row, 1964), pp. 3-6.

socially useful functions. As a result, management may have obligations to potential stockholders and to society as a whole even when
it does not have direct duties regarding actual stockholders.

Berle believes that stock and other forms of passive property
serve the following functions.[3] They can form a reserve of liquid
property to provide for old age and to free men for self-realization.
They can help to support a leisure class which can devote itself to
important social tasks which do not have a large monetary reward.
Furthermore, they provide resources for non-commercial institutional activities of foundations, universities, and the like. Finally,
the institution of passive property makes it possible to tax inherit-
ances, gifts, and capital gains.

REPORTING

Stocks and bonds can fulfill these important functions efficiently only if those who buy and sell them have adequate
information about the position of various firms in the economy.
Since management is the only group which can supply this information, we believe it has an obligation to do so. It is a social obligation to
potential stockholders and not merely a duty towards those who
actually possess at the present time. How much information should
be given is a debatable question, but as information becomes more
and more crucial, there will probably be an increased demand for it.
In theory, the annual report of a corporation, as certified by public accountants, takes care of the necessary reporting. Unfortunately,
accepted accounting principles allow so much leeway that the information may not be adequate. As Wise has pointed out in the
Insiders, three companies with identical income and identical expenses can report three widely different profit figures, depending on
the method used to record certain expenditures.[4] Some tobacco companies report taxes on sales as a part of sales, with the result that
sales are inflated while earnings as a percentage appear to be low.
Income level accounting is still not too common in reports to outsiders, though obviously management must use it for its own pur-

---

[3] Berle, *op. cit.,* pp. 47-51.
[4] T. A. Wise, *The Insiders* (Garden City, New York, Doubleday, 1962), pp.
20-38.

poses. Often when many assets are intangible or tied up in research which represents a potential asset, there is no way of knowing the true value of the company. Furthermore, from a broader social point of view, the annual report gives no information about the social costs of the business, so that it is difficult to tell whether the company really earned a profit or merely enjoyed some privilege and exploited some advantage to which it had no right.[5]

Serious students of accounting and social problems are very interested in these problems of reporting, but the public, even the educated public, is so ignorant of what is at stake that progress in this area is slow. Yet the need for more and better information is growing, and with it, the obligation to provide it. Management's concrete obligations, however, may be difficult to define. Furthermore, in the absence of uniformity or legal regulation beyond those already in force, unilateral decisions may only add more confusion. Once again we are at a point where we need broader social cooperation.

Although we cannot solve the problem completely, it should be obvious that reporting must be truthful and reasonably complete within the present system. The public has a right to know the accounting methods used and any significant definition of costs and capitalization. To put it another way, information should not only be adequate, but phrased in such a way that the ordinary stockholder can follow the report and make some intelligent judgment.

While the public accountants may develop new terminology and methods of presenting information, they cannot serve the public without management's cooperation. So long as management uses and follows accepted accounting procedures, the Certified Public Accountant must approve the presentation even though he does not agree with it completely. The norm for both groups—accountants and managers—should not be accepted principles, but rather, adequate reporting judged according to the needs of the stockholding public.

Pressure from the Securities and Exchange Commission (SEC) and the stock exchanges has done much to improve reporting. It would appear, however, that there is room for considerable improvement if management is to be publicly accountable and of service to the economy as a whole. Moreover, as we intimated in our chapter

---

[5] See Dwight R. Ladd, *Contemporary Corporate Accounting and the Public* (Homewood, Illinois, Irwin, 1963).

on secrecy, it may be that public accountability will even involve the revelation of information that has traditionally been considered the property or prerogative of only the innermost councils of business.

Realistically, reporting and revelation of data will not solve all problems. In the economic order, there are no such simple solutions. However, it must be admitted that both as a check and as a reminder of management's broader functions, better reporting has its role to play in moving the American Economy towards a more efficient and more just operation.

MANAGERIAL COMPENSATION

The increasing necessity of information and adequate reporting will serve to illustrate one of the new problems which has developed. The older problems can be illustrated in a few words about executive compensation, dividends, and the use of retained earnings.

Whether the manager is considered to have his primary obligation to the company or to the stockholder, the firm's income is not his to do with as he will. At the same time the actual relationships between managers and directors and their relative freedom from stockholder's control can give the manager broad powers which can be abused.

What are we to say of the ethics of a company which continues to pay handsome salaries to executives although operations have stopped almost completely? What principles should govern the granting of stock options which may dilute the shareholder's equity? What is to be said of generous pensions which have not been voted in advance, but are invented at the moment of retirement?

It is difficult to give precise norms for these situations. All sorts of compensations may be justified if necessary to attract and hold highly skilled executives who are in short supply. So too, industry levels may give some rough indication of what is reasonable compensation. This still leaves us with the question of whether it is unethical to pay more than necessary or more than industry levels. Actually, fairness can probably only be established by a free agreement among those whose interests are involved. This job can be done by a truly independent board of directors. It might even be done by getting stockholders to approve a formula which provides guide lines. At very least, fairness would be increased if stockholders were given full details not only about the compensation but about its potential impact on earnings and the value of stock. No matter what method is used, there should be an actual rather than theoretic accountability for decisions that affect stockholders. Once again we must face the fact that ethics can be as much a question of designing adequate institutions as of formulating abstract principles.

DIVIDENDS AND RETAINED EARNINGS

The manager's decisions about the distribution of earnings have ethical implications, for he is handling other people's money no matter what the nature of his legal rights. Perhaps there would be no problem if managers were true "economic men" endowed with lofty rationality. Unfortunately, managers are human beings with mixed motives, some of which may be at odds with sound business practices. There are managers who expand their companies not because it will be more profitable or more stable but because it flatters their ego. This is not unlike the case of the executive who invests heavily in advertising and public relations to make himself look good rather than because it is necessary for the company. Those who doubt the existence of such men should talk to the public relations expert who is given the job of making a five-foot executive look six feet tall. In addition, the personalities and irrational fears of managers will often lead them to make decisions which are safe rather than profitable. Some of the famous raiding expeditions have come about when conservative managements have created a temptation by understating assets or by piling up large cash reserves.

There is also a temptation to view retained earnings as a source of capital which entails little obligation. However, this may not be in the interest of the stockholder if he could invest his dividends more profitably elsewhere in the market. Executives, of course, tend to overestimate the profitability of reinvestment in their own firm. This, unfortunately, not only deprives the stockholder of making his own choice, but means that resources in the economy as a whole are not allocated effectively even on the basis of supply and demand.

Once again, precise norms cannot be easily formulated. However, as Schwartz has pointed out, a reasonably clear-cut dividend policy can clarify the situation. "In any event, the management should have a profitable use for retained earnings and foresee reasonable dividends on these retained earnings in the future."[6]

Much the same can be said about management decisions as to financial and asset structures. Conservatism in this area can be produced either by fear or greed. A small debt may cut down fear of failure, but it can also increase the cost of capital. So too, cash resulting from depreciation, but not used to buy new capital assets, can stagnate the firm. In short, nearly every aspect of the management of a firm's finances involves control not only of money but of fears and ambitions, when these run counter to the manager's obligations to be efficient.

These last remarks illustrate a point familiar to business psychologists, but often overlooked especially by young men in middle management. A top manager's character and values are almost as important to the efficient operation of the firm and the economy as are his knowledge and skills. Good ethics can help to build character and implement values, so that ultimately they may be responsible for a major contribution to society in spite of the fact that the opportunist and the narrow-minded individual may see them as obstacles.

RELATIONS WITH DEALERS

Like the stockholder, the dealer is generally not a member of the firm. He is, however, more closely related to it than an ordinary buyer, so that the long-enduring relationship of buyer and seller has special characteristics. Furthermore, the dealer is, to a large extent, part of the manufacturer's face to the public. It is for this reason that dealerships are so common in areas of business where a product may need a great deal of service or involve some difficult installation. The dealer on his own side, being as a rule less powerful than his supplier, is dependent for his continued existence on the supplier and his forebearance in the use of power. The ethical

---

[6] Eli Schwartz, *Corporation Finance* (New York, St. Martin's Press, 1964), p. 328. I have drawn heavily on Professor Schwartz in this section, and the reader should consult his entire chapter on Management-Stockholder Relations.

problems in this area arise not only from the relationship between buyer and seller, but from the relationship of both to the consuming public. As noted in previous chapters, the two must not enter into conspiracy against the ultimate purchaser who has a right to a fair contract of sale.

Producers have a variety of power tools which they can use in disciplining dealers. Most of these tactics are legal, but they can be unethical if used to enforce provisions or extort concessions which were not a part of the original free contract. The producer can, for example, withdraw advertising funds or financing, though this will be legal only if withdrawn from all dealers. In other cases, the manufacturer can delay shipments or fail to follow the dealers' preference. Such tactics can be extremely damaging at peak seasons when prompt delivery of reorders is the key to profits.

Dealers, of course, can provoke such retaliation by not living up to their contracts. Dealers have been known to tamper with mileage on cars so that the manufacturer's service representative does not know when a warrantee has expired. Car dealers have also been known to charge the factory for warranteed service that was not given. Some push hot items through second-hand lots and hurt other dealers.

While a manufacturer may rightly object to many of these practices, the remedy is in the courts or in refusal to renew the franchise, rather than in a kind of private penal system. Sometimes, indeed, there is need for readjustment of conditions which tempt the dealer. For example, if the factory flat rate manual for car repairs underestimates the cost of the job, the dealer will be tempted to report a higher cost repair in order to break even. So too, if the manufacturer's terms prevent a dealer from competing locally, he will try to save himself no matter what the contract says.

The old-fashioned tie-in contract, which forced the dealer to carry a full line whether he wanted to or not, is a prime example of the unjust use of power against dealers. Although such practices are theoretically illegal, in some cases the practice continues. For example, in order to obtain the brands he wants, a liquor store owner may be forced to take inferior merchandise which is difficult to move. As Sharp and Fox noted, "the fundamental law of this practice then, is that it consists of selling goods not on their individual merits but on the merits of some specialty which the dealer cannot refuse to carry and which is used to force upon him things he does not want to buy."[7] This practice also has undesirable social effects, since it insulates the manufacturer or processor from the effects of demand and forces the dealer to assume unnecessary selling costs.

A similar evil results from full line forcing where the producer is able to refuse to sell anything unless the dealer agrees not to trade with competitors.[8] While the evil of this is clear, it should be distinguished from the exclusive agency by which a given retailer has the exclusive rights to handle the product in his territory. In this case, the retailer is generally more than glad to accept the contract which does not force competition out of the territory. This is a good exchange as the manufacturer grants a valuable right in an exclusive territory, and the retailer has a real trade advantage.

At the present time there is some doubt as to the social utility of franchises, since they can be used to reduce competition. Thus the automobile manufacturers object to their dealers' selling to discounters who will force down the prices of the cars. Such control is able to cut down the savings resulting from volume·purchasing and reduce the freedom to buy a car without purchasing the dealers' unwanted services. While this issue cannot be settled in a few words, the reader should be aware that the cooperation of manufacturer and dealer can considerably reduce consumer freedom and force him to buy a joint product at a higher price.

Fair Trade prices, as previously noted, are another example of where the agreement between the manufacturer and dealer limits the freedom of the consumer by reducing the impact of competition. As is often the case, however, the steady pressure of the public which wants to purchase the product without the services will destroy the agreement unless the courts use their power to protect the so-called Fair Trade contract.

A great many ethical problems can arise when either the dealer or manufacturer violates the terms of sale. Manufacturers who grant an exclusive territory and then sell within that territory from the home office are acting unethically. Similarly, the dealer benefiting from a cooperative advertising budget offends if he pads the total bill so that the manufacturer pays more than the agreed share. This

---

[7] Frank Chapman Sharp and Philip G. Fox, *Business Ethics* (New York, Appleton-Century-Crofts, 1937), p. 30.

[8] *Ibid.*, pp. 30-35.

is merely to say that nearly everything we have said about the relationship of buyers and sellers in general, applies to the dealer as well.

SOLUTIONS

There will be fewer problems in this area if dealers combine to trade with the manufacturer. Indeed, where this has been done, or where an individual dealer is extremely powerful, the results have been more equitable. Unfortunately, the result is not always lower prices for the consumer, who cannot organize his power with the same precision and impact.

Actually, the solution may be in the provision for some form of due process through which dealers can bring complaints at a reasonable cost. At least one of the automobile manufacturers has adopted such a policy with varying success. As in other areas where there are no clear cut standards to cover many problems, due process reduces the chances of the arbitrary application and assures that judgments will not be completely unilateral.

RELATIONS WITH SUPPLIERS

The supplier, like the stockholder and the dealer, is not a member of the firm. At times, however, he may be so dependent on a particular customer or so inferior in power to the firm that special problems arise. In addition, problems arise when suppliers and manufacturers make agreements that are unfair either to competitors or to ultimate consumers. While previous chapters have covered many of these problems, a few particular problems will illustrate the type of situations which can arise.

A large department store chain is in a position to get substantial contributions to a special advertising budget by threatening to withdraw business. Such a practice is equivalent to the open or covert forcing of a supplier to assume a company's promotion costs. Similarly, a big buyer can sometimes force the financing of its operation by pushing the cost of credit back on the supplier. I know of one case where a major American company is consistently three and four months behind in its payments to a small business whose cash position is only fair. The small operator is in no position to bargain or enforce reasonable payment schedules, so that he must pay interest on money borrowed to meet payrolls and other current expenses.

Force, of course, can be used to obtain special prices, financing, and contributions, and to extort special treatment in scheduling and specifications which harm not only the supplier, but the buyer's competitors. For example, the supplier can be forced to delay the production and delivery of long-standing orders to accommodate an immediate need of the big buyer. The more dependent the supplier is on a given customer, the more likely it is for such situations to occur. Indeed, in those cases where a supplier has only one real customer, his entire operation may depend on the good will of the buyer. Ethical firms, of course, seek to avoid such situations, since they create an ethical limitation on their freedom to shift business as they see fit.

Occasionally, buyers use potential suppliers against one another by quoting fictitious low bids which will tempt the hungry supplier into the acceptance of contracts which give little profit. As noted in our discussion of contractors who bid below or very close to cost, this sort of deception can lead to the disruption of an industry and to the proliferation of cheating designed to recoup losses of the supplier. Similar deception can take place when the buyer bills the supplier for costs supposedly incurred because of mistakes on the part of the buyer. Thus a steel erector is often in a position to backcharge a steel fabricator for supposed errors, when actually the charge is being used to lower the erector's true cost as provided for in the contract. Such practices are so unethical that they hardly need further comment.

The shoe can be on the other foot when the supplier is the larger and more powerful firm, but the fact of injustice is the same. These problems, however, have been adequately treated in the chapter on the relations with buyers and in our section on the relationship with dealers.

Obviously every unfair advantage in this area harms the competitors of the favored party. The courts, for example, are suspicious of situations where a manufacturer sells to a company while buying from one of the customer's subsidiaries. Such a relationship may give the manufacturer the power to extort or simply attract reciprocal purchases from suppliers.[9] Whether the situation involves companies in related or unrelated industries, such reciprocity can give an unfair advantage to one party.

Suppliers and buyers, like other agents in the economic process, should not enter into conspiracy against the interests of third parties such as the ultimate consumer. A buyer who agrees to any price because he can easily pass on the increased costs to his customers is acting unfairly, since he has an obligation to be as efficient as possible within the limits of fairness. Furthermore, when high prices are agreed upon carelessly and with the knowledge that less efficient competitors cannot pay them, there is another example of anticompetitive practices. Often there is no legal remedy for such actions, but the unethical intentions and the harmful effects are there, nevertheless.

FOOD FOR THOUGHT

The present chapter not only raises a series of questions and illustrates the variety of problems that can occur, but points up the need for looking at actual relationships rather than at theoretical ones. Indeed, a thorough study of these areas would unearth bewildering complexities. Do the various classes of shareholders have different rights from an ethical as well as legal point of view? What are the obligations of management in the truly speculative ventures where stock is real risk capital? Do we, as Eells has suggested, need a real corporation constitution which governs its relations with all the various classes of satellites such as suppliers and dealers?[10] What problems are posed by holding companies and their control, but not complete ownership, of subsidiaries?

There are enough problems here to keep both amateurs and professionals busy for many years. These, however, are simple problems compared to those which arise because of the relationship of business to such non-economic groups as the union, the local community, and the world as a whole.

9 "High Court Finds Reciprocal Setup Is Anticompetitive," *Wall Street Journal* (April 29, 1965), p. 5.
10 Richard Eells, *The Government of Corporations* (New York, Free Press, 1962), pp. 82-88.

V

Relationship of the Firm to Non-Business Groups

13

Relations with Unions
and Local Communities

INTRODUCTION

Part Four considered the relationship of the firm to groups and individuals whose interests were primarily economic. In Part Five we must now consider the relationship between business and those groups which, while they have strong economic interests, are not exclusively economic societies. Since the interests of unions and local communities may conflict with each other as well as with those of the business community, we are dealing with an area where there is a strong temptation to use power, whether economic or political, to win the upper hand. Finally, because the relative strength of companies, unions, and local communities varies widely and changes fairly rapidly, law often lags behind reality. Even though ethics may not be able to give all of the answers, it can at least point up some of the problems and provide a few guide lines. Only time and additional study will provide more detailed solutions.

THE UNION

Although the union can be described in economic terms and be considered as a firm which controls the supply and price of labor, it is more complex than this. A union has social and political dimensions. It is concerned not only with wages, but with working conditions and with the distribution of power in the economy. It can, on occasion, be a major political force, although in the United States it has tended to play down this role. The unique nature of the union is recognized and protected in law, and although technically a private association, it is so related to the public interest that there is an increasing demand for public accountability. On the whole, however, unions still enjoy great freedom and privilege; the law assumes that they are the underdogs and seeks to equalize the power of labor and management in the hope that greater fairness will result from collective bargaining. The union, however, is not always the weaker party. Small businessmen feel threatened by the big union, while big companies and big unions have the power to make agreements which affect the welfare of consumers and weaker economic groups.

While many companies and unions have achieved a mature relationship characterized by mutual respect and broad understanding of the issues involved, this is not universally true. Indeed, there are areas of extreme antagonism and suspicion. Even those firms and unions which do get along well often indulge in flamboyant rhetoric which gives the appearance of real conflict. It is not, in short, easy to find out where justice lies in concrete cases.

ATTITUDES TOWARD THE UNION

The employer must recognize the fact that unions have a right to exist for the attainment of lawful objectives. Indeed, unions are a necessity. First, they supply the only reasonable method of working out bilateral agreements in those areas where unilateral agreements are unjust. Secondly, they provide a countervailing power which, at least in theory, should minimize some abuses.

Unfortunately, the history of unionism has seen the rise of many abusive practices and even collusion between management and labor against the interest of other parties in the economy. These abuses should not blind us to the essential legitimacy and necessity of unions. Nor should they lead us to advocate measures which cure evils only by making it impossible or difficult for the union to fulfill its necessary and useful functions. Sound attitudes, factual investigations, and discretion are obligations here as elsewhere in business life. If these are lacking in either the manager or the union leader, the relationship will develop into a power struggle which will endanger all parties involved.

"RIGHT TO WORK" LAWS

Business attitudes on the "right to work" laws indicate the existence of a real problem. The discussion of the problem is carried on with such an emotion that the ethical elements are often confused.

Any study of the question must start off with the fact that a recognized bargaining agent must, by law, operate in the interest of all workers in a plant, whether they be union members or not. This is a sound law, for if the union won gains only for its members, we could soon have a situation in which two men with the same qualifications and doing the same job in the same plant, would receive quite different compensation. Basic equity, then, demands that a union bargain for all.

Bargaining and the processing of grievances are expensive. The union, by law, must bear this expense and so must protect its financial position. As a result, unions have invested a variety of contractual relationships with employers, designed either to maintain membership or at least protect their treasury. So long as the contract is truly free, it is ethically valid, since it is in the public interest to maintain the union in a healthy condition.

It is objected that contracts calling for maintenance of membership or the check-off of dues without membership violate the right of the employee to a job. The *closed shop,* which requires an employer to hire only men who are already union members, is ethically questionable as well as illegal since it gives the union control over job opportunities and permits them, in some cases, to artificially raise wages by controlling the supply of labor. The *union shop,* which requires an employee to become a union member within 30 days of employment, does not include the evils of the closed shop. It does not limit opportunities for employment nor take away the manager's right to employ those he thinks are best qualified. The same may be said of contracts in which a man is not obliged to become a union member, but must pay dues to the union to cover the costs of union representation.

The ethical question involved in the union shop and the check-off may be phrased as follows: Are the limitations or conditions of employment an *unreasonable* interference with the freedom of a job applicant? We must remember that the applicant, if hired, will as a rule benefit from union activities. Simple equity would seem to say that he has an obligation to pay his share of the expenses. For this reason a contract calling for a check-off or for ultimate union membership appears to be quite reasonable. The applicant's right to work is not impeded in any way. He is merely required to pay for the benefits the union is obliged to provide.

In some cases it may be argued that the union shop and the check-off force the honest applicant to cooperate with crooks and undesirable people. This may well be the case, but the so-called "right to work" laws are not designed to cure the basic evils in the union itself. For this reason they are not reasonable legislation. Furthermore, the moral problem of the applicant who finds himself in this situation can be solved in a consideration of the principles covering cooperation. Finally, the individual should remember that business, too, often forces workers to cooperate with crooks and other undesirables. We do not feel this fact supports legislation which would force either business or the union to provide services without recompense.

Union busting and the systematic denigration of unions by outside propaganda should be avoided. This obligation springs not only from the demands of truthfulness and personal integrity, but also from the fact that such propaganda creates defensive postures which break down good industrial relations. Worst of all, negative publicity is often used as a substitute for the creative solution which reconciles the legitimate interests of all parties.

SWEETHEARTS FOREVER

The "sweetheart" contract, which protects the interests of labor leaders and employers at the expense of workers and customers, is so obviously an unethical conspiracy that no further comment is needed. However, a word must be said about contracts which respect the right of the workers, but harm the public good. The management that surrenders to union demands, with only a ritual show of bargaining because it can pass increased costs on to customers, is acting unethically. His power over prices, even though limited, does not absolve the manager from the duty of protecting the interests of all who depend on him. Although such situations are not covered by law up to the present time, continued abuses in this area will necessarily lead to legislation. What is at stake, then, is the economic system and not merely wages and prices in a given situation. Much the same must be said of union-management cooperation in carving up markets, eliminating competition, and in lobbying.[1]

To put it simply, if it is unethical for the management to conspire with other companies for unethical purposes, it is equally unethical to cooperate with a union for the same purpose. Unions, after all, are not exempt from the demands of ethics.

This does not mean that management-labor disputes must never force others to pay higher prices. After all, the principle of proportionality applies here as elsewhere. The public has no right to low prices which are made possible only by the existence of inadequate wages. What is to be condemned is the disregard of the public interest and the use of power to attain inflated prices. Moreover, since the line between the legitimate and the illegitimate can be difficult to determine, we are probably in need of some public guide line which has been worked out by all interested parties.

OTHER ABUSIVE PRACTICES

It should be obvious that the manager has a right and often an obligation to fight against union practices which encourage economic inefficiency, discrimination, and the limitation of the owner's right to communicate with his workers. Certain quota systems, featherbedding, and the slow-down are harmful not only to the firm, but to the economy as a whole. At times there may be proportionate reasons for allowing such situations to continue. This only means that the immediate obligation is transformed into the

[1] Bernard D. Nossiter, "Some Hidden Costs of Industrial Peace," *Annals of the American Academy of Political and Social Science*, Vol. 343 (September, 1962), p. 107.

obligation to work with trade associations and legislators for a long-range solution.

At this point, a treatise of the ethics of unions is needed to clarify all the areas of management-union relations. There appears little need to develop the point, however, since like most human beings, managers are very aware of the unethical conduct of others. What must be stressed, however, is that management cannot silently connive forever. Excuses of a serious nature do exist, but they are not permanent justifications for the tolerance of evil.

CREATIVE ETHICS

While a certain amount of tension between management and union is good, there is an obligation to see that this tension does not injure the company or the economy. To achieve this goal we need creative thinking rather than the senseless shouting of trite slogans. As Peter Drucker has noted, we also need to escape from the idea that "there is nothing objective or rational about wages, that the only criteria applicable to them is the balance of power."[2] Although completely rational and impartial decisions may be impossible, it is irrational and immoral to surrender the field to the free play of power.

The creative process demands that both manager and union escape from their old frame of reference. The manager should realize that wages and fringe benefits are gradually becoming a part of their fixed costs. Law, unions, and public opinion will not tolerate wages being considered a cost which the manager may vary at will. Social Security, Unemployment Compensation, Seniority Rights, and the guaranteed annual wage are all expressions of this attitude. Other nations, such as Japan, already see wages as a fixed cost. There are disadvantages in this attitude, but such a view would certainly motivate business to work toward greater stability in production and towards a more efficient use of its work force. Unfortunately, such a view might also speed up automation. This, however, only means that we can never escape completely from the need to balance various social values.

---

[2] Peter F. Drucker, *The New Society* (New York, Harper & Row, 1962), pp. 317 ff.

Once again the point to be stressed is the idea that there is an obligation to change those aspects of reality which force us to give less than justice to others. This is a never-ending process and one which requires imagination and the ability to escape the curse of routine thinking. At the very least, it requires us to be open to new ideas which may improve both business and the ethical conduct of human affairs. In the long run, such attitudes are necessary for survival, since the forces of society will make the change if business does not. Changes made by others, of course, may not be sensitive to the exigencies of business.

At the risk of playing the prophet, I would like to join those who see profound changes coming for labor-management relations. It is more than likely that unions will want more and more say in the management of those areas of business which affect the lives of workers and not merely their pocketbooks. While such demands may seem frightening, they stem from the realization that there is authority in the business firm which belongs to all who are involved and which has not been delegated to management. In addition, as the collective bargaining agreement has more and more implications for consumers and society at large, there will probably be demands for outside representation to protect outside rights. As labor relations become a public concern as a matter of fact, they will have to become a public concern as a matter of law.

THE LOCAL COMMUNITY

Business firms and the local communities in which they are located depend on one another. Their interests, however, are not identical nor is their power equal except accidentally. There are cases where a single firm may dominate the economy and even the politics of an area. There are other cases where the community may look on a business as a friendly cow to be milked at will. Just as businesses compete for favorable local conditions, so communities compete for new firms which will bolster their tax bases and employment figures. Since politicians are not less human than businessmen, there are even cases of sweetheart arrangements which line the pockets of owners and politicians without benefiting the community itself. At other times, the interests of a firm and a given community may coincide, but be at odds with the interest of society as a whole, of organized labor, and of other communities.

As in the case of union-management relations, society has laws and principles which cover the more flagrant abuses such as political corruption. As yet, however, we have not developed an ethic to regulate the new relationships which have arisen with the passage of time and the changing nature of both the firm and the local community. Once again then, we are plunging into a largely unexplored country.

POWER SHIFTS AND VALUES

Historically, businessmen have nearly always occupied positions of power and influence in American communities.[3] Sometimes they have used this power for purely personal aims; sometimes for the good of the entire community in which they took real pride. The same groups, which formed the company towns and kept new business out lest it increase competition, also built libraries and hospitals. Sometimes they perpetuated patterns of discrimination and segregation, but in many cases they pushed for new schools. Though the picture is not completely one-sided, the locally owned business was at least a part of the community. Its leaders shared common values and were as likely as not to be devoted to the place where they lived and worked.

Today the pattern has changed. National firms with outside managers are a part of many communities, and these have not only power but a set of interests which extends far beyond the local scene. We are, in short, dealing with a modern form of the absentee landlord. This is not necessarily evil, since many large corporations are acutely aware of the need for community relations. On the other hand, real problems can develop from such issues as plant relocation and tax increases. What makes problems difficult is not merely the fact that there is great power (this existed even when plants were locally owned), but the fact that there is a lack of any ethical consensus as to what makes the good corporate citizen.

The community involvement of outside corporations is often good but superficial. Companies encourage membership in service

[3] Richard A. Schermerhorn, *Society and Power* (New York, Random House, 1961), pp. 91 ff.

organizations, but may frown on political involvement. Hard work in the Community Chest Drive makes for real progress and a good public relations report, but it is no substitute for a fight against local corruption. Percentage contributions to local charities are laudable, but they do not make up for the failure to take a stand on segregation. At the same time, the large corporation may have good reasons for avoiding stands on more fundamental issues. It is a guest who does not want to offend a host even though the host is relatively powerless. It fears that political involvement on the part of officers who only stay a few years will not really help the community to solve its own problems. In short, because we have no completely acceptable patterns of involvement, the firm may have to steer a fairly innocuous middle course. This, however, does not change the fact that the most talented men in the community are not really a part of its inner life.

While the problems mentioned above are real, they are not so crucial as those revolving around plant relocation and the use of natural resources, since decisions and policies in these areas can have a dramatic impact on both the present and the future of the local community.

PLANT RELOCATION

A business cannot succeed without the help of the local community any more than the community can prosper without business. Because of this, continued association gives rise to a real, though vague and implied contract. Business normally expects that the local community will maintain a reasonable and orderly tax policy and encourage good labor relations. The community, on its side, assumes that business will strive to maintain stable employment patterns as well as pay its taxes and protect community resources. Although the contract between the firm and the community is not enforceable by law, it generates a real obligation on both sides, since orderly social life and community development are impossible without it.

At the same time, we must recognize the fact that both firm and community are only parts of larger economic and social units which have overriding interests. A national or regional firm is responsible to workers, suppliers, and stockholders in many communities. Even a purely local firm is often responsible to customers spread over a broad geographical area. Business, as a result, cannot make its decisions purely in terms of the local community. There are, indeed, situations where the greater good demands relocation or severe curtailment of operations in a particular locale.

Relocation and curtailment of operations based on genuine economic factors will generally be ethical, although there are problems of method and manner. At the same time, we must recognize the fact that some relocations are motivated by the possibility of *exploiting* cheap labor in other areas, or by the chance to gain an economic advantage through political power. There are even cases on record where the move was dictated by the possibility of escaping a strong union. Because such factors do exist, there is some doubt as to whether or not firms should be allowed to make relocation decisions unilaterally. Inasmuch as the public interest is at stake, it has been suggested that firms should be forced to justify their decisions before a neutral body which would decide if the move was economically justifiable. As yet, thinking on this question is not very advanced, since this is another area where the traditional market forces do not necessarily guarantee true economic progress.

Even when the decision to relocate is justifiable, the method must be considered. In addition, consideration should be given to preventative measures which will minimize the possibility of relocation hurting communities in the future.

Many of the problems can be solved if a company has policies designed to prevent imbalances. Forward-looking companies, for example, avoid becoming the dominant employer in any one region, so that strong obligations based on dependency cannot develop. Such a policy prevents a company from sinking too much money into an area and so losing mobility.

If this balance has been established, the problem of plant relocation has been minimized. The idea of balance needs to be carried into the process of relocation itself, so that harmful impacts are mitigated. The gradual phasing out of an operation gives an area time to prepare for adjustments by not upsetting the balance all at once. Cooperation with government in retraining programs or in the relocation of workers, can further soften the blow.

It should be noted that recent legal decisions are tending to limit the rights of employers in this area. Thus an employer who leaves an area to avoid having to deal with a union may be accused of an unfair labor practice.[4] We may anticipate new regulations in this area unless business is able to account publicly for its actions.

Local communities interested in maintaining economic stability must do their part to foster it. In particular, they must encourage good labor relations and provide adequate community services. More concretely, they must see to it that local housing and schools are attractive and adequate lest firms have difficulty in recruiting competent people. In many cases, the community must also provide such educational facilities as will assure both trained workers and management to local industry. Unless the communities do their part, they may be responsible for making relocation necessary.

NATURAL RESOURCES

During the great growth period of the American economy, business was able to disregard, often justifiably, the social costs of its operations. When water, timber, minerals, and air were unlimited in supply and the need for products unlimited in scope, getting the job done took first place. Today, however, as the world shrinks and the population expands, the hidden costs of business have become more obvious and the public less willing to bear them. The pollution of our streams, the poisoning of the air, the scarifying of the landscape are all costs transferred from business to the general public. In addition, the ugly plant or the shabby productive facility detracts from the community's image. These too are costs, although they appear on no balance sheet. Often even state governments are not powerful enough to legislate effective control over such abuses. Local communities have even less chance of forcing companies to bear the true costs of their operation. Ethically, however, the firm must take cognizance of these negative side-effects of its activities. Indeed, it should provide funds as a regular part of its operating expense, for the prevention and correction of such harmful effects.

---

[4] Walter E. Oberer, "The Corporation and the Rank and File Employee," *Annals*, Vol. 343 (September 1962), pp. 95-103, and James Harwood, "Top Court Upholds but Limits Right of Firms to Close to Avoid Unions," *Wall Street Journal* (March 30, 1965), p. 2.

The fact that business has not always thought in these terms does not change either the reality or the obligations that arise from it.

BY WAY OF SUMMARY

Whether the firm is dealing with the union or the local community, it should remember that neither power nor custom can justify its actions. The world has changed, and the first-class manager must recognize this if he is to act ethically and efficiently. Because the world changes, it is difficult if not impossible to catalogue all the problems which can arise. Two points, however, should be clear. First, the manager should be sensitive to the actual and potential impacts of his acts. Secondly, he should look to cooperation rather than conflict as a means of solving problems which arise in his relationships with groups of unequal power. This cooperation itself should not take the form of a conspiracy which exploits unrepresented third parties, but should look for the creative solution which, by rising above the traditional and known, finds a level where all interests can be more perfectly harmonized. At times, it may even involve legislation that will protect honest companies and third parties from power plays and politics.

Although some will say that these suggestions disregard the true nature of business, I believe that they indicate what business will be and must be if it is to fulfill its mission. Equally important, they indicate the challenge and satisfaction which the businessman can gain if he sees his work in a broader perspective. Indeed, as we shall see in the final chapter, the new mission of the businessman may involve changed attitudes towards the whole of the economy and the world itself.

14

Business
and the Social Economy

INTRODUCTION

The past few chapters have raised issues of social importance and posed problems which cannot be completely solved by individual firms or even by the business community as a whole. It is time, then, to take a look at the ethical problems of the business system itself. While there is no room for any full treatment, a glance at even a few issues will help to clarify the ethical challenge which faces business in the twentieth century.

Ethics is concerned with judging the suitability of means to the end. If a means does not serve the end or serves it at too high a cost, we cannot ethically continue to use it. Moreover, if there are alternative means that serve the end with less cost, that is, with fewer harmful side effects, good ethics obliges us to abandon our present course of action. Our business system, like the Constitution of the United States, or even a system of family organization, is a means, not an end. It is neither a sacred cow, nor an ultimate value. It is a tool to be reevaluated in terms of the goals it is supposed to serve. The system itself is controlled by firms and the firms, by individuals. In the last analysis, men must do the evaluating and make the changes necessary to bring the system more closely into line with the changing needs of men and the society of which they are a part. As we have noted again and again, this responsibility cannot be avoided, although often it is transformed into the duty of doing what can be done at a given moment. After all, there can be no excuse for not looking at things as they are rather than as we would like to believe they are.

THE PARADOXES OF THE AMERICAN ECONOMY

We live in the richest nation in the history of the world. Our gross national progress staggers the imagination even as it continues to grow. Both our per capita and average family income are so high that all other nations appear to live in abject poverty. We have huge quantities of cars, telephones, bath tubs, and television sets, and yet, we live in a nation where poverty and at times even deprivation continues to exist on a fairly broad scale. The "other America" of which Michael Harrington writes actually exists, even though the experts may quibble about the exact point at which a family is considered to be poor.[1]

The existence of this poverty is paradoxical, since we have excess capacity and idle manpower in both agriculture and business. Indeed, the very efficiency of our economy and the brilliance of our technological advances help to create poverty by making workers obsolete at the same time that they create new goods which can satisfy human needs. Strangely enough, people are often in the position where they can buy luxuries such as a television set, but cannot get necessities such as good housing. Even at the risk of appearing to agree with everything in Galbraith's *The Affluent Society*, it must be admitted that children who live in good homes must go to substandard schools, while only the fairly well-to-do can afford all the medical care they need.[2] Moreover, anyone who has traveled in the much poorer nations of Europe will admit that our cities lack much of the charm and beauty which one would expect to find in a wealthy nation. The traveler who has visited Holland, Sweden, or Switzerland will also have to confess that there is nothing to equal our rows of slums which are like great unsanitary prisons.

[1] Michael Harrington, *The Other America* (New York, Macmillan, 1962).
[2] John K. Galbraith, *The Affluent Society* (Boston, Houghton Mifflin, 1958).

In point of fact, then, the United States appears to have refused to use its resources to satisfy the private and public needs of its citizens. It has made progress, to be sure, but the system has not really used its riches to good advantage. This failure cannot be explained except by saying that we have refused to admit the problem and have hesitated to attack it with full vigor.

HIDING THE PROBLEM

Although social critics have publicized problems for generations, the general public has not always faced them. Many never have any contact with poverty, since it is found in geographic and racial pockets. Others who do meet it face to face often reinterpret it to suit their convenience. Thus, poverty is interpreted to be either a temporary state which would disappear or the result of shiftlessness. In addition, the picture of the good life is so well publicized by advertisements and the movies that there is little room left for news of poverty except at Thanksgiving and Christmas.

Our public poverty is easier to disguise. Most of our people have limited ways of comparing their present state to something better. Indeed, even our better educated people are sometimes very poor judges of the quality of the education being given their children. If you are used to ugly cities, it is difficult to criticize them. If you are used to thinking of your public services as the best in the world, it is impossible to realize that they may be very poor indeed.

Even when we have admitted the existence of such problems as poverty, we have not faced them. We have been persuaded that time would work things out. We have been told that government intervention would be too expensive or too dangerous. We have been convinced, in fact, that the world was really all right despite appearances to the contrary. The great depression and the thirties dispelled many of these ideas and the nation made some progress, since it was realized that the ordinary mechanics of business and the competitive system could not solve all problems. This, however, was crisis activity and the old mentality has continued to blind us to many problems.

THE MYTH OF COMPETITION

Not merely the existence and nature of poverty, but the true nature of our economic system are mysteries to a large part of our population, including a large part of the business community itself. Many small businesses do exist in a world of rather real competition in which no one seller can really influence prices or the allocation of resources. Since there are a number of these businesses, both their owners and friends constitute a large group believing in the existence of a competition which automatically assures that justice is done. Such ideas are, of course, reinforced by superficial courses in economics as well as by Fourth of July orations and the publications of the National Association of Manufacturers.

Students of the economy, of course, have been well aware that the small business does not set the tone of the economy. Big business does that, and big business has had the power to escape much of the discipline of the market. As a result, it has often been able to set prices and allocate capital in a way that was not envisaged by classic economic theory. These very groups have an interest in maintaining the myth of competition since this helps to quiet the nerves of the populace. They have even coined such misleading terms as "People's Capitalism" in order to turn attention from the real centers of power in the economy. This fact of tremendous power in large concerns is generally concealed by another set of slogans which extol free enterprise, the American system, and other vague but emotionally attractive concepts.

This fact of power must be acknowledged by the individual. One must be aware of the influence of economic concentration on the political and public sphere. As Bernard Nossiter has pointed out in *The Mythmakers,* the President's Business Advisory Council is largely dominated by big business.[3] It has, moreover, given advice that has often been more profitable to its members than to the general public. Even President Kennedy discovered that it was not easy to discipline big steel, and he quietly backtracked when they made things too hot for him. This political influence is not merely the

[3] Bernard Nossiter, *The Mythmakers* (Boston, Houghton Mifflin, 1964), pp. 3 ff.

result of political contributions and memberships on government committees. It also rests on the work of lobbies, who do a good and not necessarily dishonest job of representing the business position to Congress.

Big business and its trade associations are aided by small business in protecting the public mind from contamination by reality. There are committees which scan school books to make sure that they do not deviate too much from the picture business wants to present. There are foundations which run programs for clergymen in the hope of teaching them a simple and favorable picture of the economy. There are newsletters available to educators which further inculcate a simplified and comforting picture of the system. I cannot say exactly how effective all of these efforts are. However, I find that the old myths are pretty well embedded in the thinking of my students and even in the economic philosophy of many college professors.

I do not wish to imply that businessmen are either vicious or stupid in fostering these myths. Many of them are true believers who have never stopped to question the system. Others are so busy that they do not have the time to examine the reality of the world in which they live. Still others feel that they are only countervailing forces struggling against the unions, the reformers, and crypto-socialists. My point is merely that we must face reality and discover if it is really serving our goals.

THE TRANSCENDENTAL MARGIN

The myths of universal affluence and of the competitive system are reinforced by the idea that our economic progress, limited though it is, has been due to a business system that is profit motivated. This, to be sure, is the major reason for not rocking the boat or criticizing the goose that laid the golden egg. In point of fact, however, much of our progress not only in production but in the just distribution of economic goods has been due to the modifications which we have made in the system and in what Berle calls the transcendental margin.[4]

[4] Adolph A. Berle, *The American Economic Republic* (New York, Harcourt, Brace & World, 1963), p. 202.

"The transcendental margin is the product of a value system that causes effort and expenditure beyond that calculated as conducive to the personal advantage of an individual or his immediate family group. Development occasioned by such a value system does not exclude, but rather includes, use of the state and its agencies in mobilizing and applying effort and expenditure. But its effect is never limited to state measures and actions. The aggregate of such effort, expenditure and sacrifice over and above the aggregate of effort and expenditure for such personal desires is the added coefficient that causes national product to increase beyond satisfying the aggregate effective personal desires of the population."

These statements mean that the United States has improved both the productivity of its economy and the distribution of its wealth by devoting much of its resources to areas outside the profit-motivated economy. They mean that we have used gifts, foundations, and private organizations of a not-for-profit status to improve the lot of men and, indirectly, the efficiency of the productive machine. They mean that the government has increasingly been a factor in production as well as in redistribution.

Many men do not want to face these facts, for they show that an increase in non-market activity and a decrease in market power may be the clue to progress. Worse yet, they may indicate that all of the propaganda against these changes may be a real disservice to the nation and even to the economic side of business.

PROFITS AND SOCIAL COSTS

If we accept the fact that both growth and progress have stemmed from a mixed system, it follows that profit may be a meaningless concept to use in the evaluation of the social performance of a firm or of the business sector of the economy. When much of the productivity is due to the results of education, profit may represent the surplus created by society rather than by the business system, or it may be that profits can be viewed as money which the firm did not expend because it did not pay all operating costs. Smog, industrial odors, pollution of rivers, shortened lives, and nervous tension are all costs of production paid by society and private individuals even though they are not shown clearly on the balance sheet of any corporation.

Social costs are represented not only by the scars of strip mining and the burning coal pile which threatens to undermine a town, but by the effects of the working wife on the home and the education of children. As we have already mentioned, the travelling husband who cannot fulfill his duty as father may also represent a social cost. We do not know exactly what business does cost us nor what it gives us. Perhaps we can never know with complete accuracy, but we must make some attempt to find out if we are to evaluate the system as it is and not as it is imagined to be.

ECONOMIC DISLOCATION
AND STABILITY

Some time ago the United States decided that the cost of instability was too high and adopted government measures designed to mitigate fluctuations and their effects on workers. The work of the Federal Reserve Board in balancing credit, the effects of Unemployment Compensation on dropping purchasing power, and Federal Aid to depressed areas are all designed to reduce the cost of the free market system. Urban renewal programs have also helped in improving housing when the private economy proved incapable of doing the job in time. Businessmen are not always happy about these plans which limit their freedom and their power in many ways, but most will admit that the programs have benefited both business and the general society. The question remains, however, as to whether or not we have done all that we can to reduce the cost of instability without harming the essential mechanisms of a free society. Do we need to stabilize the use of consumer credit which has been responsible at least in part for some of our recessions? Do we need to extend the coverage of unemployment insurance? Do we need a hundred other measures to control inflationary forces which benefit the debtor but impoverish those with fixed incomes?

The problems of instability are being compounded by dislocations resulting from changing markets, changing technology, and the resulting cultural lag. The blessings of automation are liable to bring us new unemployment at the same time that they obsolete equipment and increase our over-capacity. The new economy demands new skills at a time when many students to not finish even high school. Plant relocations to meet new markets and to take advantage of lower labor costs can leave whole communities gasping for life. All of this takes place in a nation that already has depressed areas and a considerable body of unemployed and poor. As yet, we have not developed a way of attacking these problems on a global and continuous basis. The costs of dislocation are high, and we must ask if the system needs to be readjusted to reduce them.

NEW CONCEPTS AND NEW VALUES

Automation creates the possibility that more and more goods will be produced with less and less manpower. If anything, it will aggravate the problem of abundance, since the increase in production creates a problem in distribution. Even the businessman recognizes the fact that increased capacity may be self-defeating unless income is so distributed that large numbers can buy the new fruits of the business system. At this point, the attempts at a solution are complicated by the problems of definition and evaluation which, while they may seem very abstract and philosophic, must be solved if we are to act intelligently.

The businessman would like to solve the problem of excess capacity and abundance by teaching people to fill their new leisure with consumption. *Consumption is thus elevated to the status of a virtue,* if not a patriotic duty. Others, however, see leisure as the time a man can use to be a man with or without consumption. These thinkers see the possibility of an age in which men have time to cultivate the mind and the spirit as adults and not merely while they are children in school. They see the possibility of increasing unpaid services in areas where there is real need. *Consumption is no virtue* for these and may even be a vice if it keeps man from doing more important things.

A change in our concepts of the nature and value of leisure involves a change in our idea of work. If leisure, or time during which we have a chance to be men, is more important than consumption, then work becomes not so much a means of earning a living and buying things, as a means of transforming the world and developing one's own personality. In such a world, a man would not be judged by how much he had, but by what sort of a person he was and by how much he had contributed to society. A change in our concept of work and leisure would involve a change in evaluation which would relegate the entire business system to a less important place in our society. This is not pure theory, for many societies, some of them rich and highly cultivated, have adopted a similar point of view.

Businessmen are not used to thinking in such philosophic terms, for they are men of action. Yet action is guided by our values and not merely by blind urges. In the last analysis, it is our idea of the good life and the value of the individual which controls everything that can be controlled. It seems to me, then, that ultimately business may have to face the problem of ascertaining the relative value and meaning of work, leisure, and consumption.

RELATIONS WITH GOVERNMENT

Although the deeper issues raised above cannot be solved by any one agency, it should be obvious that many of the questions can be answered only in terms of a new form of cooperation between business and government. This relationship has grown in time and will continue to grow both in extension and intensity. This is necessary, for we are in a time of transition. It is also inevitable, for as economic power increases, the relationship between it and political power becomes more and more crucial. As MacIver has noted, the problem cannot be solved merely by deciding on the proper and exclusive field of each power.[5] The two spheres, as they must, interact.

Up to the present time, business has often insisted on viewing government as an enemy. The businessman fails to admit that any good can come out of Washington, lest he compromise his own position. Instead of entering into rational discourse with the government and society as a whole, he often hopes for a sort of high school debate which aims not at the truth, but at victory. While the interest of business and government may not always coincide completely, the continuance of warfare or, at best, heavily armed neutrality will not solve the problem.

[5] R. M. MacIver, *The Modern State* (London, Oxford University Press, 1926), pp. 291 ff. See also John F. A. Taylor, "Is the Corporation Above the Law?," *Harvard Business Review*, Vol. 43 (March-April, 1965), pp. 114-130.

When the businessman does enter the political arena, it is all too often as a politician who would manipulate the machinery of government for his own purposes. Only a few have adopted a statesman-like posture and looked for creative solutions. These are hard words, but the ideas have been drawn not so much from the enemies of business as from the thoughtful writings of men within its own ranks.

If the businessman is to make his full contribution to society, he must first realize that he is no longer the simple huckster who is tolerated, if not despised, but rather, a member of the new aristocracy. It may be an aristocracy of power, money, and intelligence, but it is still informed by the principle of *noblesse oblige*. The obligations are not always easy to define, but a few examples will illustrate some areas where I believe they do exist.

LOBBYING

Lobbying is, in general, not only a legitimate but necessary activity in our country. Unless legislators are carefully informed of the facts and various points of view in a given society, they cannot legislate wisely. Truthful informative lobbying should be encouraged. Lobbying, however, conjures up images of bribery, conspiracy and pressure as well as the use of phony front organizations and various forms of blackmail. The unethical quality of most of these acts is so clear as to need no commentary. Indeed, the major problem may not exist in these areas at all.

The real difficulty is probably in the non-creative nature of much lobbying. Often, where there is a real political problem, business seems to be concerned not so much with helping to solve the problem, as with maintaining the status quo or receiving special protection. As a result, necessary social reforms are often neglected while business generally ends up in a worse position than it would have been with a truly creative solution. When lobbies are used for such purposes, one has doubts about business ethics even though the offense cannot be nicely classified in traditional ethical categories.

I have often been surprised to find men of good will lobbying against bills designed to remedy real abuses simply because these men possessed an inherent dislike of government, or because less honorable men had made it unpopular to support virtue publicly. Often, to be sure, the man of good will feels that self-regulation can do the job since he charitably endows others with his own integrity. Perhaps, it is merely an unconscious fear that the admission of some faults in the industry will encourage others to denigrate business and supply unfair critics with ammunition. No matter what the explanation, the refusal to cooperate for a higher good is hardly the stand of the good citizen who realizes that there are times when personal advantage must be sacrificed to a higher end.

My point can be exemplified by the opposition of business not only to the unreasonable portions of the truth in the packaging bill, but to any bill even though it might help business itself. On one occasion I heard an executive in an important packaging firm attack the bill, although he could not specify one objectional provision in it. He impressed his audience with the irrationality of his position and left them with the suspicion that he had not studied the bill at all. It is this sort of opposition which hurts both business and society.

A similar lack of cooperation is sometimes found when the Federal Trade Commission asks for aid in developing standard terminology. As well as serving to police borderline operators, the development of trade guides can help and protect the honest manufacturer and retailer.

Honesty forces one to admit that the government sometimes has too many officials who are bent on crusades and on making a name for themselves. Often too, one can detect a note of hostility and a lack of understanding of the businessman's problems. Some agencies leave major points so vague that the businessman does not know where he stands. Others are tempted to use detailed blueprints where none are required. It would appear that before we can make real progress in this area, there will be need for an ethic of government. The problem, however, will not be solved by continuing to accept the present relationship as definitive.

PLANNING

Many of the real problems in the American economy cannot be solved without cooperative planning in which government, business, and consumers have a role. Yet planning is an unsavory socialistic word to many businessmen. This is paradoxical, since the businessman himself is an expert in planning and builds his future on careful study and organization. Why, then, does he object to introducing the same rationality into the economic system as a whole?

To some extent, the opposition springs from a fear of government. Also, as Bunting has noted, planning would take the fun out of the market game and the pleasure out of profits.[6] Profits, after all, are supposed to be a sign of success and a justification of business power. Planning would change the public meaning of profits and take away some of the glory from the businessman. To put it another way, the businessman may recognize that planning involves not merely increased efficiency and government intervention but a change in the meaning of business and in his own status.

It must be admitted, however, that planning is increasing elsewhere in the world and with considerable success. Furthermore, as Nossiter has noted, planning may be a necessary means of protecting our own basic values and of assuring a more efficient allocation of resources.[7] Actually, our economy is already characterized by a great deal of planning and seems to have profited from it. Planning, moreover, does not mean government control, but cooperation with government. At best, it is the systematic study of means and ends. As such, it can even be consistent with free enterprise, although not, of course, with *laissez-faire* or rugged individualism. In many cases, it involves the presentation of information and the use of persuasion in order to perfect the working of the market. It can thus leave the essential outlines of existing institutions relatively untouched in many cases.

While national planning is done under the auspices of the government, the control group can and does include representatives of business, the public, and the union, so that the will of the people will be more perfectly reflected in the choice of goals. The execution of those goals, however, must still be left to managers.

Although it is difficult to assess the success of planning in the non-Communist world, even conservative economists admit that it

[6] John R. Bunting, *The Hidden Face of Free Enterprise* (New York, McGraw-Hill, 1964), pp. 110 ff.

[7] Bernard D. Nossiter, *The Mythmakers* (Boston, Houghton Mifflin, 1964), pp. 193 ff.

has not restrained progress. At the very least, plans seem to create an atmosphere of confidence which promotes innovation and risk-taking. In many cases, plans have helped business to reduce the number of contradictory government policies and even to anticipate technical, material, and labor shortages in particular fields. Planning may also help to cut down investments which might lead to excess capacity.

While it may be impossible to take a definitive stand at this time, it seems difficult to imagine an America which cannot utilize the best of planning without sacrificing its basic values, even though some of the old folkways may have to be eliminated. Indeed, I suspect that even on the rational level, our national genius can equal if not surpass that of the French, the Germans, and the Swedes, who have done a great deal with far less resources than we enjoy.

INTERNATIONAL

When business ventures into international markets, it is a representative of the United States. Since the businessman is a citizen, he thus assumes certain obligations. After all, economic imperialism is as bad as colonialism as far as our foreign policy is concerned.

The problems of the American businessman are doubly difficult, for he not only represents the United States, but he must also deal with businessmen and governments often riddled with corruption. As a result, he must be particularly astute both as a businessman and and as an ethician. Frequently indeed, he will find that he must use the ethics of the lesser evil. In nations where the bribe is considered a normal part of an official's income, the fiduciary relationship is a bit different, and as a result, its violation may not have all the evil effects which would follow in the United States. One does not like to be in the position of countenancing less ethical social institutions, but often we must accept what we cannot change so long as we do not will the evils involved. This will most certainly shock the purist, but it is quite consistent with the principles developed in the first chapter of this book.

In many of the developing countries, not merely government but business itself is corrupt and exploitative. Although the American businessman cannot come as a reformer, he should be on his guard against adopting local attitudes which are often not only un-ethical, but uneconomical as well. No one likes to be a rate-breaker, but some American companies have found that paying a living wage increases their productivity even though it may irritate the local "robber barons." In any event, the American businessman should not allow moral blindness to dominate his own thinking.

Possibly the most difficult cases will arise when sound business practices conflict with the national goals of the United States. Thus, Ford's investment of some three hundred and sixty million dollars in England certainly had an adverse effect on our balance of payments, even though it was a very profitable business maneuver.[8]

Businessmen, unfortunately, have not always responded to the requests for voluntary cooperation, but this fact may only lead to increasing government controls. Once again, the issue involves the ability of the business to discipline itself in the interest of a greater good. And once again, the issue is broader than the immediate prob-lem, for the structure of whole system is at stake.

The problems of corruption abroad and of cooperation with American policy should not obscure the real challenge of the devel-oping nations. These countries lack capital and managers. Often they lack the means to raise the capital and train their own execu-tives. As a result, whether they lean to the West or to the Communist world, they need what American business has to give. It may indeed be that American business which is truly creative can do more to assure peace and freedom than all of our armed forces. Business and commerce have always been civilizing influences. Today they have a chance to be major forces for world peace.

IN CONCLUSION

This final chapter has probably left some readers bewildered and other readers angry. It is not practical in the sense of being narrowly pragmatic. It may be condemned by some for it questions existing institutions and labels. Nevertheless this chapter

---

[8] Charles E. Summer, Jr., and Jeremiah J. O'Connell, *The Managerial Mind* (Homewood, Illinois, Irwin, 1964), pp. 85-116, give an interesting collection of data and opinion on this case.

is a necessary part of any book in business ethics that is not concerned with mere regulations, but rather with the development of the creative function of business as a part of the broader society. Anyone with imagination will see that the realization of these ideas presents a challenge to the business community. Business is asked to see itself as a part of the mainstream of American life with something more important to contribute than what appears on a balance sheet.

The writer hopes that business will undertake this significant task, for it alone has the techniques and knowledge necessary to translate ideals into realities. Indeed, in the measure that business does meet the challenge, we can expect to find that our nation prospers and our freedom grows as an inspiration to the rest of the world.

A Bibliographical Note

The notes given with each chapter can serve as a very brief bibliography. The following published bibliographies which complement one another will provide reading for a lifetime.

Robert Bartels, ed., *Ethics in Business* (Columbus, Ohio, Ohio State University Press, 1963) , pp. 137-180. Thomas M. Garrett, *Brief Classified Bibliography in Business Ethics* (Scranton, Penna., University of Scranton Press, Institute on Business and Social Ethics, 1964). Philip W. Van Vlack, Charles L. Sewrey, and Charles E. Neilsen, *Economic Ethics Bibliography* (Brookings, South Dakota, South Dakota State University Press, 1964) .

In a field that is growing rapidly, the latest developments must be followed in the periodicals. I recommend both the *Harvard Business Review* and *Business Horizons* for their continuing treatment of the broader questions of social ethics in business. *The Wall Street Journal* is necessary reading for anyone who would keep pace with the day by day developments in business and its legal regulation.

Both the Center for the Study of Democratic Institutions and the National Conference of Christian Employers and Managers publish interesting studies on various phases of both individual and social ethics in business.

Index